Lifeline for the End Times:

Creating a New Humanity During the Apocalypse

and Beyond

LIFELINE FOR THE END TIMES

Creating a New Humanity
During the Apocalypse and Beyond

Peter R. Lawson

★

WEST COUNTY PRESS

Cover and interior design by Rebecca Dwan. Cover and interior
illustrations are details from Albrecht Dürer (1471–1528), *The Seven
Trumpets Are Given to the Angels* (1497–1498), woodcut from the
Apocalypse series.

With great foreboding and outrageous hope
I dedicate this book

To those among us who will be most endangered
by the impending apocalypse:
the children of the world especially,

William Michael,
Iris Olivia,
Mason Roe,
Parker Daniel Jason,
Annette Grace,
Henry Falcon

Contents

Preface

"It's time to check out when I am not contributing more to the life of the world than I am taking from it." That's what I decided about 20 years ago and now I think I may be in peril.

I set about writing this book because I do need to contribute more to the life of the world. Should you, my gentle reader, take the time to read the book you will decide the matter. Is *Lifeline for the End Times* contributing enough to the life of the world to match, or hopefully, exceed what I'm draining from the life of the world?

There is a measure of the useless feeling called guilt involved in this project. Guilt is useless because it tends to immobilize us, and we don't need passivity. I feel responsible for not doing enough to hold off the oncoming tide of the multiple disasters that are destroying humanity. I don't expect that you or anyone else will forgive me. I am not asking for forgiveness. I don't want you to join me in my irresponsibility. I am asking you to do something.

Start by doing this. Take a hard-hearted look at what you and your children and your children's children will be facing in the rest of this century. Then act now in such a way as to provide them with the best tools, the best knowledge, and the best wisdom to not only survive, but to thrive as civilization crashes around them. As you read on, I hope you will find at least a few tools, and some knowledge and wisdom for the time of the apocalypse.

I have had five careers so far. The first was as a student. The second was as a parish priest and churchman, which is to say I was involved in the apparat of the church as well as in the local parish. My third career was as a high-level political staffer in a gubernatorial campaign and then as an organizational and management development consultant. My fourth career was back in the ministry, and my fifth career is making retirement worthwhile.

As I look back on this series of adventures, the underlying pattern can be described as expeditions into organizations and institutions, trying to manipulate them into being more healthy and humane. In my fourth career back in the church, I was particularly focused on undermining the hierarchical structure of the church so that it might become an egalitarian community focused on love and trust. Unfortunately, the social function of the church in civilization is to gather people around a divine sanction of the domination/violence system. The church's hierarchical structure replicates and validates domination. Violence only emerges in religion when its shadow side is exposed.

This book presents some of the things I have learned during my adventures. As we move further into this catastrophic century, I hope that what you read will be of some help to you and to your children and your children's children.

There are parts of this book that you will not enjoy. Remember that I didn't write it to entertain you. I wrote it for our children, our grandchildren, and their children.

Acknowledgements

I am one of those lucky ones who can honestly be thankful to my parents for the way they raised me. They made me feel very secure and at the same time gave me encouragement and support to roam away from home and into adventures that few of my peers experienced. They, more than anyone or anything, stimulated my lifelong curiosity about what was really happening behind the social conventions and the structures of common life.

After college I studied at Yale Divinity School where my mentor and friend, the late John Oliver Nelson, was Director of Field Education. He labeled me as one of a handful of his "square pegs." He called us that because he thought we would never fit into the round holes of the church. He helped me accept my role as a professional with one foot in the church and one foot kicking against its dysfunction and institutional inertia. Accepting myself as a square peg also enabled me to be comfortable both thinking and working outside the box.

I am very thankful for all of the people in my life who have had a major impact on my thinking and whose influence is foundational in my work. I can single out some who were particularly important. Walter Wink turned me on to the domination/violence system. Peter Drucker introduced me to the impact of the Neolithic revolution. Kenneth Boulding led me to understand the dynamics of technological revolutions. Peter L. Berger introduced me sociology in general and the sociology of knowledge. Kurt Lewin founded the National Training Laboratory. My participation in its Group Life Laboratories was my experiential introduction to the dynamics of groups and organizations. Saul Alinsky, founder of the Industrial Areas Foundation, electrified me in a single two-hour seminar and taught me and so many of us about community organization. Jack Gibb taught me the power of love and trust in one experiential weekend workshop.

I give special thanks to John Dominic Crossan, Marcus Borg, and Jack Spong, who energized my liberation from Christian doctrine and validated my devotion to the Historical Jesus whose radical teaching undermines the domination system and models egalitarian community.

I thank Lynice Pinkard and Huey Newton, whose work led me to conceive the notion of evolutionary suicide.

I thank all the scholars and writers whose work is cited in the book. Please take the time to Google them to learn what more they have to say about the state of the world and life during and after the Sixth Extinction.

I have deep gratitude to those who made significant contributions to *Lifeline for the End Times* as I was writing it and sending it out to them chapter by chapter, especially three of my most helpful critics and supporters, Harry T. Cook, Mike Short, and Marta Illueca, MD. Without them my writing would have more serious shortcomings than it does.

I owe a debt of thanks to folks who read each chapter as it was written and who commented from time to time pointing out errors and omissions. They kept urging me onward. Notable among them are Elizabeth Curtis, Anne Gross, Nicholas Jones, David Hoffman, David Anderson, Gene Kirkham, Mary Ann Marshall, Harry Coverston, Marika Szgethy, Cathleen Gerwig, Mike Mallers, Rex A. E. Hunt, Nancy Donahue, and Mike Siegel.

I am dependent on the ongoing support of my friends and fellow "philosophers" John Gallagher, Jim Turner, and Bill Newmeyer, who contend with my thinking month after month.

My special thanks to designer/copyeditor Rebecca Dwan. She designed the cover and text, refined the title, suggested editorial changes, and shepherded me through the complexities of publication.

Most of all I am grateful to my powerful wife, Danielle, and our heirs, Kris, Elizabeth, David, Matt, and Ruth. They are the six most important people in my life. They fill my affective domain with their love and continue to teach me the things they know that I need to know.

Finally, I give thanks for the wonderful host of relatives, friends, and colleagues whose companionship on the Way has been an immeasurable gift.

I hope all of you will find yourselves honored by your role in my work.

Thank you all.

Introduction

Late November 2014

The indications are that life on planet earth in the next century will be in peril. To say that may be putting a rosy glow on the possibility of catastrophic devastation for all sentient life.

How shall we deal with that kind of a future?

Lifeline for the End Times is my modest answer to that disquieting question.

I'm starting with this assumption, namely that you believe that adults have a major responsibility to raise children who are competent enough to not only cope with the exigencies of life, but to overcome them.

Your oldest child is five. Your youngest child is two and a half, or your oldest grandchild is five and your youngest grandchild is two and a half. Have you thought about what the next 35 years will be like for children who are just beginning school? Have you thought about what life will be like when your oldest child is 40 and your youngest child is 37½?

I know what life is like for parents of young kids. I've been there and done that. We had five children in seven years and there wasn't very much time for lying around reading magazines and eating chocolates. That's why I won't hold you at fault if you haven't had the time or energy to think seriously about your children's futures.

The reason I wrote this book was to help parents and grandparents to prepare themselves and their children for the world to come. I wanted to lay out a picture of what the present portends for the future of humanity and to offer some very basic strategies for creating supportive human communities that can discover and nourish grace, beauty, and goodness while the world around them is in chaos.

The earth itself is diseased. A host of experts have been studying its symptoms and projecting diagnoses. Most of them do not see much hope for life on earth as we have known it. They think the disease is irreversible global warming. They believe that the combination of a capitalist world economy, a fossil-fueled extractive infrastructure, and the unwillingness of people and politicians to seriously consider major social, economic, and political change are doing irreparable damage to the world's ecosystems.

I do not disagree with the experts. Like them I believe we have come to the end times. Unlike many writers, however, I don't believe the cause of our demise is simply global warming. Global warming is but one symptom of the root disease.

I believe the earth and its people are suffering from a malignant disease at the core of civilization itself. The disease is the domination/violence system and it has become so universal and so toxic that it is incurable.

The signs of terminal disease are everywhere. If you have any doubts that our civilization is dying or that it is, indeed, sick, I suggest that you turn to Part One (chapters 1–6) and read it carefully with an open mind. It may scare you. You may, as some of my readers have already expressed, be upset and dismayed by the evidence that I present. I believe, however, that you *do* need to be frightened by what is coming about in our sorry world. If you are disturbed by Part One, I will have accomplished part of my task because I want you to be concerned enough to enlist in the cause of creating a community of love and trust in your immediate circle of friends and neighbors.

On the other hand, if you are fully convinced that the situation in which we find ourselves is very grave and irreversible; if you find yourself in the company of people like Bill McKibben, Elizabeth Kolbert, and Naomi Klein, I suggest you go immediately to Part Two and begin reading what I propose as some foundational personal and group skills and strategies to preserve and protect us through this century and to lay the foundations for a new humanity in the post-civilized era.

Underlying much of what I've written is my skepticism about a fundamental assumption that virtually everyone makes. The assumption is that the true nature of human being became manifest during the first major technological revolution in the Neolithic period. Tribes of nomadic, hunter-gatherer peoples characterized human culture before the agricultural revolution. After that revolution humans became settled citizens of new urban areas. For 10,000 years we have believed that a settled citizenry in a hierarchical social system was the apotheosis of human evolution.

I disagree or at least I differ in my understanding. In Chapter 8 I look at the difference between genetic evolution and mimetic evolution. There was a slow genetic change when the basic human diet shifted from a so-called Neolithic diet to a diet based on grains. After the agricultural revolution humans became smaller in stature and developed larger skulls. (It may not be safe to assume that larger skulls meant more mental capacity.) Memes are the cultural equivalent of biological genes. Mimetic evolution directs changes in human society. Mimetic evolution has proceeded through three more technological revolutions until today when the memes of civilization, that is to say, the memes of a culture of hierarchy, domination, and violence continue to shape human culture.

I suggest that our primitive forebears, those nomadic hunter-gatherers, may have had a set of memes that we would do well to understand and embrace.

I need to be honest with you. I don't have any academic credentials or a significant body of work to give credibility to what I have written. All I have that validates my work is a history of skeptical thinking and looking outside the box to find answers to the conundrums, the idiosyncrasies, the tragedies, and the glories of human existence.

In Chapter 8 I also present what may be a new concept. I call it evolutionary suicide. It is the process of dying to the memes of civilization so that new memes can direct social life and social structures. Since civilization is dying it is no great loss to precede it to its demise. Evolutionary suicide is a radical act that involves not only death but rebirth. Rebirth is a complex process of growth and learning very like the experience of infancy, childhood, and adolescence. What I have tried to do in Part Two is lay out some foundations for what will be an intense period of learning and discovery. Among other things, you will need to plunge into learning about the skills of living close to and dependent on nature without the benefits and curses of living in a world dependent on fossil fuel.

Given my limitations, there is no way I could have begun to lay out the pathways for all of that. You are more than competent to do that yourselves as the conditions of life lead you. I think there are suggestions enough in Part Two to build a curriculum that a small dedicated community can study and practice.

I wish you Godspeed on your spectacular and awe-inspiring journey.

And how are the children doing?

Part One

Chapter 1

The malignant disease of civilization

WE HUMAN BEINGS are in one terrible mess. Things had looked better and better for the last 10,000 years. We made progress over the centuries. We no longer live in caves and run around in the woods gathering up good-tasting weeds or hunting for meat with a club and a spear. Unless we are impoverished, we live in grand houses cooled in the summer and warmed in winter. We eat well. We have an abundance of available food, picking up our groceries at Whole Foods or Walmart, or driving out to McDonald's or Thomas Keller's newest bistro. Our clothes aren't made of skins. Most of them are made with synthetic fabric made from petroleum pumped out of the ground. We are the beneficiaries and victims of "Better Things for Better Living—Through Chemistry."[1]

Among the world's peoples I am most privileged. I am living very well as an American and I live in an abundant society. I'm not a one percenter or a two percenter, but compared to most others, I am at the comfortable top of the heap.

I am not happy, however, about where and how I live, because I think I am in the last generation of my family to have it so well. I think my children, now all in middle age, my grandchildren, and their children will live in the end time for our civilization and its benefits. My great-grandchildren are in the fifth of the seven generations we should be looking after. We have not thought about protecting any of them from our excessive appetites and our overreaching search for power and wealth.

Life on earth, at least for those of us in the developed nations, has been a great ride up until now.

All the wonderful stuff that now makes our lives much easier is a result of our creativity. We figured out how to dominate and manipulate the natural world to meet our selfish ends. As long as it has lasted, we have been all too eager to collaborate in the rape of the earth.

We found ways to suck the oil out of the earth and mine coal by scraping off the tops of mountains. We learned how to refine oil into fuel for our factories and mills, and for our ubiquitous vehicles. Coal was the perfect fuel to melt iron and make steel. Coal and oil generated most of the electric energy to light our homes and power our appliances. We can now see what we have done and we know that we are verging on catastrophe.

In the last 20 or 30 years we have realized that burning coal and oil has enshrouded the earth with atmospheric carbon dioxide, which has changed the climate. Now we know how the shroud melts glaciers and causes the oceans to rise inch by inch. Climate change is the disastrous byproduct of our great industrial technology. We have been living in a carbon economy. It will not last and we will again live in cold houses.

Environmental degradation is only one of the crises we face. The continuing rape of the earth and the terminal abuse of its peoples are being driven by global predatory capitalism, a more daunting and probably more significant contribution to the great mess of the twenty-first century.

4

At one time the world's most powerful corporations were all trying to embody the Christian God, according to Bruce Brown in his *History of the Corporation*.[2] But Dr. Brian Moench says this:

> Needless to say, in the 21st century, corporations as creations of civilization make no pretense of embodying the Christian God. In fact, today, corporations come much closer to embodying Mary Shelley's Frankenstein than Jesus Christ. Ironically, created by and managed by humans, corporations have become almost robotic monsters, perpetrating, even feeding off human misery, threatening every aspect of human life—the air we breathe, the water we drink and the food we eat—and even the future of mankind itself. What have these corporate Frankenstein monsters done for us lately?[3]

Moench goes on to cite the callous lack of concern about human life when the garment factory in Bangladesh collapsed, as the political power of gun manufacturers has defeated gun safety legislation, and the decades-long obfuscation and deliberate lying by the tobacco industry about the addictive nature of tobacco which has killed so many. He also cites the long-time use of lead in all kinds of products long after it was known to be disastrous for human brains. Now we can add to the list Monsanto and their genetically modified organisms as well as the pharmaceutical industry encouraging the rampant use of antibiotics in animal products. The death certificate of all the victims over the years should read "Death by corporation."

As they say in infomercials, "But wait! There's more!" We now have a new phenomenon: an alliance between the corporations and government at every level. It is now Death By Corporatism.

It is too depressing to document all the ways that governments have allied themselves with corporations to dominate our culture and society. Two examples will have to suffice. The first is ALEC: the American Legislative Exchange Council.

Here is what ALEC has to say about its history and work.

More than 30 years ago, a small group of state legislators and conservative policy advocates met in Chicago to implement a vision: A nonpartisan membership association for conservative state lawmakers who shared a common belief in limited government, free markets, federalism, and individual liberty. Their vision and initiative resulted in the creation of a voluntary membership association for people who believed that government closest to the people was fundamentally more effective, more just, and a better guarantor of freedom than the distant, bloated federal government in Washington, D.C.

To date, ALEC's Task Forces have considered, written and approved hundreds of model bills on a wide range of issues, model legislation that will frame the debate today and far into the future. Each year, close to 1,000 bills, based at least in part on ALEC Model Legislation, are introduced in the states. Of these, an average of 20 percent become law.

For more than 35 years, ALEC has been the ideal means of creating and delivering public policy ideas aimed at protecting and expanding our free society. Thanks to ALEC's membership, the duly elected leaders of their state legislatures, Jeffersonian principles advise and inform legislative action across the country. Literally hundreds of dedicated ALEC members have worked together to create, develop, introduce and guide to enactment many of the cutting-edge, conservative policies that have now become the law in the states. The strategic knowledge and training ALEC members have received over the years has been integral to these victories.

Since its founding, ALEC has amassed an unmatched record of achieving ground-breaking changes in public policy. Policies such as teacher competency testing, pension reform, and Enterprise Zones represent just a handful of ALEC's victories in the states.[4]

In other words, ALEC writes laws that are made available to legislators in the several states and are enacted most often by Republican-dominated legislatures. ALEC isn't the only culprit in this process. The people we elect to positions of power in government cannot be fully informed about the complexities of many of the problems they are asked to deal with on a day-to-day basis. ALEC provides knowledge and expertise to develop laws that benefit corporations on issues that cannot be fully understood by legislators from Oshkosh and Millville. Given the intellectual limitations of many elected officials, many legislators could not write the laws they conveniently accept from ALEC.

The second example of the collusion between government and corporations involves Monsanto and the Senate Agriculture Committee in crafting legislation to benefit Monsanto's proliferation of GMOs. A dangerous provision was appended to the budget bill passed in Congress in March 2013. Without any hearings on the matter, the Senate included language that requires the U.S. Department of Agriculture to essentially ignore any court ruling that would otherwise halt the planting of new genetically engineered crops.

Here is how Andrew Kimbrell, executive director of the Center for Food Safety, described the situation:

> In this back-room deal, Senator Mikulski (D, Maryland) turned her back on consumer, environmental, and farmer protection in favor of corporate welfare for biotech companies such as Monsanto. The new provision makes what is currently discretionary or optional on USDA's part, mandatory. The word "shall" forces the USDA to continue allowing biotech crop cultivation even if its commercialization was overturned by a court.

By sneaking Section 735 into a federal appropriations bill, Monsanto successfully planted a dangerous provision in U.S. law which strips judges of their constitutional mandate to protect Americans' health and the environment while opening up the floodgates for the planting of new, untested genetically engineered crops.[5]

We do not need to be reminded about the impact of the military-industrial complex on our entire government. It has reached new pinnacles of malfeasance that have been revealed by the work of Edward Snowden. He has opened up the vast and probably unconstitutional intelligence apparat of the NSA, which makes George Orwell's *1984* seem like a garden party. Orwell could not have imagined the intricate abundance of "intelligence" available to the NSA on the World Wide Web.

Greed has triumphed not only among the predatory capitalists, but also among the hoi polloi who from their regions of deprivation aspire to be wealthy and powerful. Our culture is steeped in a pathological addiction to the excesses of imperial civilization, a toxicity that puts humanity on a downward spiral to an earthly hell.

The autoimmune disease that is killing our civilization is the domination system.

The domination system is not new; it arose in concert with the beginnings of written history.

The domination system is the core principle of civilization; the foundation upon which human progress has been built and which is now self-immolating, carrying us along.

It is a hierarchical system based on violence.

In a domination system the most violent and powerful rulers or elites oppress others to enhance and further their self-interests.

The apocalypse wrought by civilization is upon us.

8

We turn next to look more carefully at the birth and history of the domination system.

---

[1] Mid-century advertising slogan of DuPont Industries.

[2] Bruce Brown, *The History of the Corporation,* Volume One, BF Communications Incorporated, 2006, CD-ROM (out of print).

[3] Dr. Brian Moench, "Mankind: Death by Corporation," Truthout, op-ed Wed., 26 June 2013.

[4] From ALEC's web page, July 2013.

[5] Adapted from Michelle Simon, March 28, 2013, copyright © 2013 TheHuffingtonPost.com, Inc.

Chapter 2

A little (rough and simplified) history

I WASN'T PRESENT when humanity first manifested its terminal autoimmune disease during the first great technological evolution. It took place a bit before my conception, ten thousand years before, more or less.

I'm talking about the exponential technological shift for humankind from hunter-gatherer cultures to the culture of settled agriculture; the beginnings of civilization and its attendant domination system. There have been two (some scholars say three) more technological revolutions in our history. We look at revolutions three and four a bit later. For now we want to look at the origins of civilization.

A rough analysis of the history of civilization begins with the development of settled agriculture in the Neolithic era, 10,000 to 8,000 BCE. During this period people in all the major river valleys of the world discovered that daily hunting and gathering could be replaced by much less laborious work. It is easier to plant crops in rows and enclose feral animals that can be fed with cultivated grains. As settled agriculture became more successful, it was necessary to build granaries to preserve surplus grains. Granaries led to urbanization, to cities inhabited by many folks no longer directly engaged in procuring their daily nourishment.

Inevitably, cities and granaries became bait for marauders from nearby hungry communities. So some of the surplus citizens, the former hunters and gatherers, organized themselves to guard the granaries against the predators. The guards eventually became organized into *proto-armies*, led by the most violent leader (lo, a King is born). Some of the other surplus hunters and gatherers became bean counters, i.e., accountants who kept records, wrote things down, and became scribes. Other scribes became artisans, priests, and theologians. Theologians, clever then as now, became very valuable because they invented and validated the notion that the Leader/King was a living representative (and incarnation maybe) of the prevailing God(s).

From those beginnings arose the social structure of city-states, of civilization. Civilizations are characterized by a number of elements that were evident in the incipient societies in the fertile river valleys around the globe. The elements were settled agriculture, defined trade routes and transportation systems, writing, currency, legal systems, and occupational specialization that included metallurgy, architecture, science, art, organized religion, and most significantly, a political structure. The domination and exploitation of natural resources is not mentioned as a characteristic of early civilizations even though the depletion of natural resources is an element that leads to the decline of societies and cultures.

The *domination system* was the political structure of early civilization. In the beginning it was simply the militarization of towns and cities.

The social and political structure of civilization under the "domination system" has a simple social contract at its core, with both the "Leader" and "Followers" adhering to a basic covenant (or set of agreements), as follows:

12

The Leader (the most violent male?):

I, the leader, will set the rules. You will follow and obey the rules, and I will care for you, protect you, and bring you into a land flowing with milk and honey.

The Followers:

Since we are weak, afraid and want security and to live in your beneficent land, we will be loyal and obey you.

The Leader:

The Gods have decreed that we shall organize a hierarchical system of power. I will be at the top.

You will be someplace below me. I'll be in charge of where you are in the system and what benefits you get. Your role in my hierarchy of power and privilege will depend on two things:

1) How productive you are for me, and,

2) How obedient you are to me.

If you cause too much trouble, I will withhold my beneficence from you, or punish you or kill you.

American sociologist Gerhard Lenski developed this diagram to depict the social structure of early civilizations.[1]

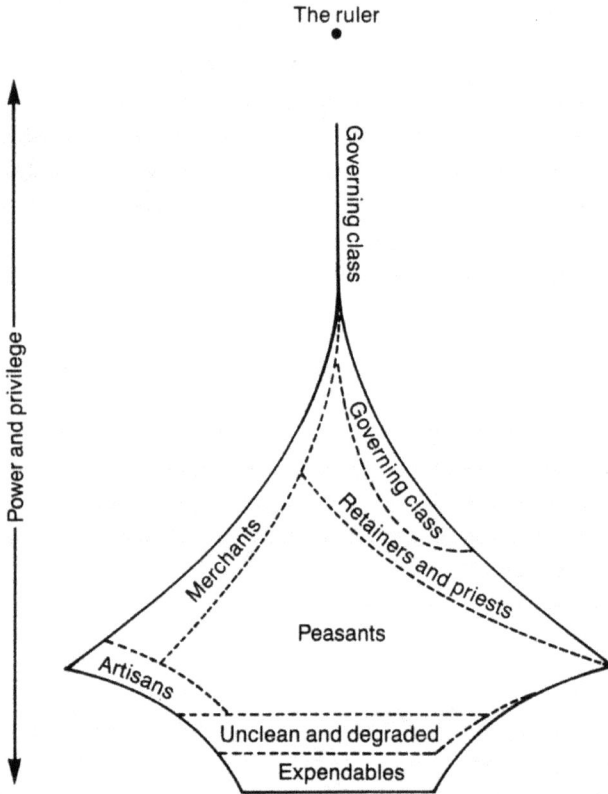

Biblical scholar and theologian Walter Wink has said,

The domination system is characterized by unjust economic relations, oppressive political relations, biased race relations, patriarchal gender relations, hierarchical power relations and the use of violence to maintain them all. No matter what shape the dominating system of the moment takes (from the ancient Near Eastern city/states, to the Pax Romana, to feudal Europe, to communist states, to fascist, or state capitalism, or

14

to modern market capitalism), the basic structure has persisted now for at least ten thousand years, since the rise of the great conquest states of Mesopotamia around 8000 BCE.[2]

Peter Drucker was a renowned writer, professor, management consultant, and self-described "social ecologist" who explored the way human beings organize themselves and interact in much the way an ecologist would observe and analyze the biological world. He has said that there has been no basic change in the structure of society since the Egyptian army came into existence in about 6,000 BCE. That was his conclusion in the 1950s well after the second great technological revolution.

The Industrial Revolution was the second exponential technological change in human society. The oceanic social changes brought about by this revolution were begun by some relatively modest technological changes that led to new ways of thinking about the nature of things. Christopher Columbus (1451–1506), Nicolaus Copernicus (1573–1543), and Galileo Galilei (1564–1642) are men who come to mind because their achievements changed the way people conceived of the earth and universe. They opened the way for a revolution in thinking characterized by the application of thought to the explanation of natural phenomena. Sir Isaac Newton (1643–1727) is the most recognized philosopher and mathematician of those whose lives and works initiated science, a whole new way of thinking. The scientific revolution and new philosophical movement, the Enlightenment, lay the groundwork for those of a practical mind to tinker with their ideas about mechanics.

The Industrial Revolution was also fueled by an abundance of capital. The governing class, the nobility, owned mines and vast tracts of agricultural land. Their wealth gave them a level of leisure so that some of them applied serious thought to the reorganization of the means of production. They invested in the manufacture of goods. They built hand-work factories powered by water and horsepower, and later, steam engines.

Technologically, the industrial revolution may be said to begin in 1712 with the invention of the first steam engine by Thomas Newcomen. He built an engine to pump water out of coal mines. Nearly a half century later, James Watt developed a vastly more efficient model that began operating commercially in 1776.

In the late 17th and early 18th centuries, wool production evolved from a cottage industry to water powered mills. Mills with coal-powered steam engines could be built far from the rivers and streams that had once been the only source of power. In 1814 George Stephenson built the first portable steam engine that hauled freight and passenger carriages on iron rails. The railroad was a powerful enhancement to early industrialization.

While technology was beginning to make gigantic changes in the way people lived, the hierarchical domination system developed at the birth of civilization carried over quite nicely to the industrial era.

Has there been a third and a fourth technological revolution? Historians offer several different options to categorize the technological and social changes have taken place in the last 200 years. There's no doubt that technological changes have changed society and culture. Maybe a third technological change began with a change from sailing ships to steam powered ships, and vast new networks of railways. Maybe it began with the invention of the internal combustion engine with cars and trucks, and the development of oil and gas extraction. Maybe it began with the development of atomic energy, and jet engines in space travel. There are some students of technology who suggest that there has been a fourth revolution, the Digital Revolution when digital technology overtook analog and mechanical processes. They would suggest that the Digital Revolution marked the beginning of the Information Age, a change analogous to the Agricultural Revolution and Industrial Revolution.[3]

No matter how these changes are categorized or identified, each of the technological changes that differentiate one era from another has had a remarkable effect on the social dynamics of civilization. Each new era sees changes in the means and distribution of sustenance, of labor and work, patterns of urbanization, trade, economics, and communications systems. The basic political and social structure, the domination system, stays much the same despite the variety of names and forms given to the historic period.

Although I missed the first one, I was born at an opportune time to experience some of the tag-end relics of the Second Industrial Revolution and participate in the beginning of the Information Age.

My immigrant grandfather, Carl Ernfred Lawson, was a carriage builder, and a very successful one. There was nothing he could do, however, when the internal combustion engine overwhelmed his business. The horse and carriage was on its way out in 1903, and when Henry Ford introduced the assembly line for motor vehicles it was all over. Some relics of that era did survive long enough for me to experience the very last days of the horse and wagon.

As a kid I lived in New Britain, Connecticut. During the 1930s, in the depth of the depression, a horse and wagon came down the street about once every six weeks. The driver we called the Ragman yelled out, "Rags, ah rags." When they heard him, some housewives would come out with worn-out clothing, towels, sheets, and other rags that they sold to the

Ragman for 15 or 20 cents. Our milkman drove his horse and wagon down the street delivering bottled milk to his customers. I can remember being amazed that the horses stopped as soon as he dropped the reins and that they stayed still until he picked up the reins again.

During World War II, during my teens, I worked on the Parmalee dairy farm in Durham, Connecticut. The farm was not mechanized. We worked with horses and wagons. Most of my job was out in the hayfields with the other hands pitching hay on to a "hay-rick," a wagon pulled by a two-horse team. The horses hauled the rick back to the barn where we distributed the hay evenly into the hayloft.

I also saw a bit of the last days of steam power. During a break from my student days, I worked as a dock-builder for the New England Dredge and Dock Company repairing and building docks in New Haven Harbor. Our crew worked on a lighter, essentially a large barge with a tall crane aboard. The crew consisted of the foreman (captain), the crane operator, the fireman, and two or three of us riggers. The crane, capstans, and pile driver aboard the vessel were powered by a steam engine. The fireman's job was to shovel in the coal, fire up the boiler, and get the steam pressure up to working level. The rest of us couldn't do much work until the engine was at full steam. I think our lighter was powered by the last steam engine functioning on a daily basis in Connecticut, if not in New England. Most of the other rigs in the business had diesel engines by then.

When I was a neophyte curate at Trinity Church in Southport, Connecticut, I had the great good fortune to meet and come to know Colonel Harry DeLyne Weed as a friend. Locally he was best known for planning and supervising an unusual project. The church was situated on land subject to flooding in extreme high tides. Col. Weed had the church

18

jacked up and then set down again on 18-foot concrete walls with huge footings. Nationally, Col. Weed was better known for having made significant impacts on industrial life. As a young machinist working in a bicycle factory in upstate New York, he was the first person to electrify a manufacturing facility. During the First World War, he invented the mechanism that enabled machine guns to fire through the propellers of fighter planes. He also invented the horizontal bomb rack that changed the nature of aerial bombing.

In the spring of 1983 I bought an Apple IIe computer, two or three months after it was introduced. That computer was my first venture into the Information Age, into computers and, later, the Internet. I have been swimming along in that stream for 30 years now and I love every minute of it. I especially enjoy the ability to sit here dictating a first draft of this stuff. After it's saved on my hard drive somewhere, and/or out in the cloud, I can go back in a day or two and rewrite it. I can sit here shifting back and forth between dictating and searching for material that I have gathered up for this book, or that I need to find to keep myself honest.

I am thankful that I was able to witness the end stages of the technological transition from agrarian-based civilization to industrial-based civilization. It is now virtually complete in every continent, and even the so-called underdeveloped nations are moving with electronic speed into the Information Age. All the once tribal, rural and agrarian cultures in the world are now citified, i.e., civilized, except for a few tribes buried deep in South American and East Asian jungles.

Through the power of multinational corporations and a world economy, the autoimmune disease built into civilization is now manifest in every country in the world. Now nearly every person on the planet suffers either directly, or from the side effects, of the fatal disease at the heart of civilization: the domination system.

Let us next bring it up to date—Domination in the Information Age.

---

[1] Diagram is from Gerhard Lenski's *Power and Privilege: A Theory of Social Stratification*, copyright 1984 by the University of North Carolina Press; used by permission.

[2] Walter Wink, *The Powers That Be: Theology for a New Millennium* (New York: Galilee-Random House, 1999), p. 39.

[3] http://en.wikipedia.org/wiki/Information_Age

Chapter 3

Bringing it up to date—the domination system in the information age

I WAS IN THE FOURTH GRADE in 1937 when the information age began. That year Claude Shannon, a graduate student at MIT, wrote a master's thesis that demonstrated the possibility of digital circuit design and digital computers. He later went on to publish a landmark paper that has made him the "father of information theory" and one of the great men of our time. His work laid the foundation of the digital and information revolution.[1]

Shannon's accomplishment was accelerated into a world-changer with the development of the transistor, the integrated circuit, and the silicon chip. Those innovations miniaturized the essential components of all the digital electronic devices we rely on every day. Now there are chips everywhere; in the alarm clock that jars me awake in the morning, probably in my toothbrush, in the microwave, in my iPhone, and in a few years, maybe one in my ear.

You've probably had experiences of the information age very like mine. I continue to be amazed by the devices developed over the last three decades. We were having dinner one evening with our granddaughter Rae, her husband Mike, and their three-year-old son Will. Will finished up his mac-and-cheese and for a few minutes played with the crayons and small toys that his folks had brought. When Will got bored Mike gave him his cell phone. He was no longer bored. I asked Mike what he was doing on the phone. Will was erasing pictures of himself that he didn't like. Mike laughed, and told us how he had noticed some charges from the App Store that didn't seem to be things he had ordered. He found out that Will had been buying games and installing them on the phone. At three years old, Will is too young to remember when the information age began. A few years later a similar scene unfolded when Will's younger sister, Iris, age 22 months, took over her mom's iPhone. Iris was searching the phone for our favorite songs and playing them while we finished our pizza.

I'm amazed when I can sit at my computer planning a trip to London, knowing not only how to get from our hotel to Charing Cross Station on public transport but learning the precise times at which the bus will be leaving the stop across from our hotel. Everyone these days wants a home office. My wife is a realtor, and when she does a home search a requirement of every client is space for a home office. That's as true for people who don't work at home as for those who are liberated from a cubicle down at the word factory and can work online. All of us can sit at a computer and manage all our financial transactions.

The unfortunate part of our doing our banking online is that we have had to deal with an obscenely big bank that was instrumental in busting up our economy. Our bank was one of those that was "too big to fail."[2] Capitalist bankers have learned how to use information age technology to run rough-shod over their customers while gathering in enormous piles of cash for themselves. Now, thankfully, we have moved our business to a local credit union.

I challenge you to come up with any aspect of our life that has not been radically altered by information technology. I also challenge you to find any significant place where the predatory capitalist oligarchs who make up the top 2% of our population do not use it to amass more wealth and power and control information technology.

We need to be clear. The domination system in the twenty-first century information age is not presided over by a king or emperor (at least in the West). It is presided over by a small cadre of oligarchs who share a common culture.

Who are the capitalist oligarchs who rule the world?[3]

In context, overall, the *richest 400 people* in the US have as much wealth as 154 million Americans combined; that's 50 percent of the entire country. The top economic 1 percent of the US population now have a record *40 percent of all wealth*, and have *more wealth than 90 percent* of the population combined.

To get into the top economic 0.01 percent (one-hundredth of one percent) of the population (in the USA), you have to have a household income of over *$27 million* [15] per year.

These are some of the guys who are among this Economic Elite group:

Former Goldman Sachs CEO and Bush Treasury Secretary Hank Paulson had already amassed at least $700 million prior to moving to the US Treasury in 2006.

Current Goldman Sachs CEO Lloyd Blankfein and a few other top executives at Goldman Sachs just received $111.3 million in bonuses. Blankfein just took home $24.3 million, as part of a $67.9 million bonus he was awarded.

Goldman's President Gary Cohn took home $24 million, as part of a $66.9 million bonus he was awarded.

Goldman's CFO David Viniar and former co-president Jon Winkelried both took home over $20 million in bonuses.

If you think people in this income level don't control the US political process, you are not paying attention. After they caused this economic crisis, they got the government to give them trillions of dollars in taxpayer support, and then, after taking our tax dollars, they gave themselves all-time record-breaking bonuses. 2009 was an all-time record-breaking year for Wall Street executives, bringing in a total of *$145 billion*. And then, in 2010, they raised the bar even higher, breaking the all-time record set the year before by pulling in another *$149 billion*. The audacity of it all is stunning.

Finding people more grotesquely greedy than Wall Street executives would seem to be impossible.

Unlike those in the lower half of the top 1%, those in the top half and, particularly, top 0.1%, can often borrow for almost nothing, keep profits and production overseas, hold personal assets in tax havens, ride out down markets and economies, and influence legislation in the US. They have access to the very best in accounting firms, tax and other attorneys, numerous consultants, private wealth managers, a network of other wealthy and powerful friends, lucrative business opportunities, and many other benefits.

The dramatic increase in economic inequality and poverty, along with the unprecedented rise in wealth within the top one-tenth of one percent of the population has not happened by mistake. It is the designed result of deliberate governmental and economic policy. It is the result of the richest people in the world, and the "too big to fail" banks, using the campaign finance and lobbying system to buy off politicians who implement policies designed to exploit 99.9 percent of the population for their financial gain. To call what is happening a "financial terrorist attack" on the United States, is not using hyperbole, it is the technical term for what is currently occurring.[4]

The essential quality of the ruling oligarchy is privilege. Privilege is defined as a special right, advantage, or immunity granted or available only to a particular person or group of people. Oligarchs claim a right to be greedy. They claim a right to take advantage of all the best things in life. They are immune from prosecution for any number of crimes against the people. As I write this, it is impossible to identify any corporate leader or banker who has been indicted for criminal behavior.

The predatory capitalist oligarchs live in a walled-off, private, Trumped (sic)-up cultural oasis where their sealed-off society pretends to live in the real world. Their goals and values are deeply embedded and they recruit ambitious, talented people into their ranks, converting them to their way.[5] They also seduce the rest of us into serving their needs, as we shall see.

Al Gore is (or was) a town crier about climate change and a sometime Democratic senator and presidential candidate. He has moved a long way into the oligarchy. This is from George Packer's article "How American Society Unravelled After Greedy Elites Robbed the Country Blind" in *The Guardian,* June 2013.[6]

> Earlier this year, Al Gore made $100m (£64m) in a single month by selling Current TV to al-Jazeera for $70m and cashing in his shares of Apple stock for $30m. Never mind that al-Jazeera is owned by the government of Qatar, whose oil exports and views of women and minorities make a mockery of the ideas that Gore propounds in a book or film every other year. Never mind that his Apple stock came with his position on the company's board, a gift to a former presidential contender. Gore used to be a patrician politician whose career seemed inspired by the ideal of public service. Today—not unlike Tony Blair—he has traded on a life in politics to join the rarefied class of the global super-rich.

It is no wonder that more and more Americans believe the game is rigged. It is no wonder that they buy houses they cannot afford and then walk away from the mortgage when they can no longer pay. Once the social contract is shredded, once the deal is off, only suckers still play by the rules.

The social structure of the oligarchic form of the domination system is much the same today as it was in monarchies of early civilization.

The contemporary form of oligarchy requires only symbolic and replaceable heads of state (e.g., so-called monarchs, presidents, or prime ministers). There is no need for an Emperor. The oligarchy is a collaboration of the wealthiest élite, the top 2 percent. It does, however, require cadres of retainers. As Gerhard Lenski has pointed out, the élites need the support and loyalty of retainers. The wealthy top 10% are the predominant retainers in our oligarchy. Under them, and not necessarily well paid, the bureaucrats doing the daily work make up the vast majority of retainers.

These armies of bureaucrats serve a corporate system that will quite literally kill us. They are as cold and disconnected as Mengele. They carry out minute tasks. They are docile. They are compliant. They obey. They find their self-worth in the prestige and power of the corporation, in the status of their positions, and in their career promotions. They assure themselves of their own goodness through their private acts as husbands, wives, mothers, and fathers. They sit on school boards. They go to Rotary. They attend church. It is moral schizophrenia. They erect walls to create an isolated consciousness. They make the lethal goals of ExxonMobil or Goldman Sachs or Raytheon or insurance companies possible. They destroy the ecosystem, the economy, and the body politic and turn working men and women into impoverished serfs. They feel nothing. Metaphysical naiveté always ends in murder. It fragments the world. Little acts of kindness and charity mask the monstrous evil they abet. And the system rolls forward. The polar ice caps melt. The droughts rage over cropland. . . . The sick die. The poor starve. The prisons fill. And the careerist, plodding forward, does his or her job.[7]

Along with the bureaucrats, the military, politicians, law enforcement, athletes, and entertainers[8] are also caught up as retainers to the ruling class.

Another phenomenon in American culture serves to reinforce the dominance of the oligarchy. Many Americans who are living month to month and carry inordinate amounts of personal debt honestly believe that they will soon become millionaires. So they have little interest in changing the system. "Less than 1 in 20 American households has a million dollars, but 2 in 10 Americans believe they'll become a millionaire in the next decade, according to an AP-CNBC (2011) poll."[9]

Recall the covenant in Chapter 2 between the first king and his people. That first thug may have had the longest spear. The technological innovations of the Industrial Revolution and the Information Revolution have changed the equation. The spear has been replaced by digital intelligence, surveillance, and weaponized drones. The élites are screening your phone and computer, checking on your loyalty and obedience right now. The covenant that began the domination system has been revised. Now the oligarchs and their hosts of co-conspiring élites say, "We have drones and we have 'intelligence' on every one of you, and dissension is domestic terrorism. Be obedient, or else."[10]

New technologies, for all their alleged benefits, have placed engines of power in the hands of the predatory capitalist élites who we are only beginning to recognize. The ruling élites now have control of all the weapons of power and are morally bankrupt.

We now turn to look at some manifestations of the Apocalypse.

---

[1] Claude Elwood Shannon (April 30, 1916–February 24, 2001) was an American mathematician, electronic engineer, and cryptographer known as "the father of information theory." http://en.wikipedia.org/wiki/Claude_Shannon

[2] Much to our satisfaction, we now do our banking at a local credit union.

[3] Richard (RJ) Eskow calls them the Superpredator Corporate Class. Romney and the Rise of the Corporate Superpredator Class www.huffingtonpost.com/rj-eskow/romney-and-the-rise-of-th_b_16231. . .

[4] Alternet, August 11, 2011, "Meet the Global Financial Elites Controlling $46 Trillion In Wealth." An adapted excerpt from David DeGraw's new report on the financial destruction of the United States. The full report can be read here: Analysis of Financial Terrorism in America.

[5] People ask what changed Obama from the man who ran for the presidency to the man who has been president. The answer is, I think, that his background was plebeian, which made him naïvely unaware of the culture of the ruling oligarchy. Once in office, he was caught up in their web of influence and power and adopted their ways.

[6] http://www.alternet.org/news-amp-politics/how-american-society-unravelled.

[7] Chris Hedges, July 23, 2012, in Truthdig.

[8] Who else to provide the endless circuses that numb the minds of the people?

[9] "Two in 10 Americans expect to be millionaires within a decade," Laura Clawson, Mon. Sep 19, 2011, Daily Kos Labor.

[10] "Be Careful What You Google: Music Writer Says SWAT Team Raided House Based on Harmless On-Line Browsing," AlterNet, Aug. 1, 2013: "NSA in action? Joint Terrorist Task Force searched house based on innocent Googling of backpacks and pressure cookers, couple says." www.alternet.org/civil-liberties/nsa-action-writers-house-raided-based-innocent-google-search

Chapter 4

The apocalypse is upon us

THE MOVIES PROVIDE ample evidence that the apocalypse is upon us. Four apocalyptic movies were released in 2013. *World War Z* starring Brad Pitt is perhaps the most well known. The story line: a United Nations crisis expert leaves his family to combat a global zombie pandemic which threatens to destroy humanity. After the US opening on June 21 the worldwide gross was $375,056,920. Did they come to see Brad Pitt or see the world end?

Here are the other apocalyptic films:

This Is The End is a comedy about some stoner friends who throw a self-indulgent house party. Outside the apocalypse begins as strange catastrophes devastate Los Angeles. As the world outside collapses, the six friends are inside, trying to deal with the oncoming end of the world as we know it. Holy Smoke!

Rapture-Palooza is based on the fundamentalist fictions about the apocalypse. The rapture happens while a young married couple are bowling and suddenly there are empty shoes under piles of clothes as the saved, the believing guys are lifted to heaven. Then the two survivors become engaged in a battle with the Antichrist. Holy cow!

In *Pacific Rim* the apocalypse begins when Kailua, monstrous creatures, begin rising from the sea starting a war to destroy humanity. To combat them, civilization creates massive robots called Jaegers. Holy Moly!

> *WWZ* . . . evokes the hectic density of modern life; it stirs fears of plague and anarchy, and the feeling that everything is constantly accelerating. At times, it has the tone and the tempo of panic [an anthem that is played regularly on Faux News]. [Are zombies] the embodiment of what we might become if we let ourselves go—soulless vessels of pure appetite, both ravaged and ravaging? Do they represent our apprehension of what hostility lies behind all those blank faces in the office, at the mall, across the dinner table?[1]

Does the "Z" represent the psychological apotheosis, the ultimate state of our shadow side that no Roman numeral could signify?

2012 was a far bigger year for apocalyptic fantasies than 2013 because of widely circulated nonsense about the Mayan calendar predicting that the world would end on December 21, 2012, by any number of bizarre events involving planets that don't exist or other meteorological and gravitational hallucinations.

Apocalyptic extravagance obviously sells movies and video games. People are buying because they are fascinated with end-of-the-world scenarios. Fictional monsters from the deep, zombies, and satanic emissaries are psychologically much easier to manage than the issues that threaten humanity in the real world. A cancerous disease, the domination/violence system run loose, is causing the rapture of the coming apocalypse, which will be the end of civilization, if not the end of the world.

Some of the more scientifically reasonable doomsday scenarios of apocalyptic movies are at best remote possibilities and far beyond any human agency to prevent. Think of a massive comet or asteroid striking the earth like the one that wiped out the dinosaurs 66 million years ago, or a huge volcanic eruption that blankets the earth with ash and obscures the sun for decades. Such scenarios are a modern take based on our increasing knowledge of the earth's history, but they were not in the consciousness of people of the pre-scientific world.

Apocalypticism has emerged as a theme in art and literature in most periods of human history when there have been dramatic changes in the social order. Albrecht Dürer's *Apocalypse* series, for example, was produced in 1498 as a manifestation of the widespread fear that the world was ending in 1500. A school of apocalyptic poets was prominent in the World War II era in Great Britain. The best-known apocalyptic work, the Biblical Book of Revelation, continues across time to be a stimulant for wild speculation about the end of history and the return of the Christ to rule the earth.

The root of the word *apocalypse* is Greek and means uncovering or revealing. The Revelation of John is an elaborate dream sequence uncovering the divine secrets of the end time, when the good (Christ) triumphs over the bad (the Roman emperor). Its symbolism is incomprehensible to many and is, therefore, a ripe ground for many interpretations. It is a theological Rorschach blot.

The use of the term apocalypse today implies a convergence of phenomena that are leading to a collapse of the social and natural world as we have known it. Apart from the movies, video games, and end-time fiction, other forms of apocalyptic apprehensiveness are appearing in the media focusing on the fragile state of the environment and the collapsing social and economic structure.

For example, Robert Jensen has published a very short book, *We Are All Apocalyptic Now: On the Responsibilities of*

Teaching, Preaching, Reporting, Writing, and Speaking Out. He argues that the world and its people are threatened.

> The systems that structure almost all human societies produce profoundly unjust and fundamentally unsustainable results. We have both a moral obligation and practical reasons to work for justice and sustainability.

> Progressive analyses of inequality and injustice focus on the illegitimate hierarchies in patriarchy, white supremacy, the imperial nation-state system, and capitalism. The final hierarchal system—and in some ways the most dangerous—is the industrial model of human development, the latest and most intense version of an unsustainable extractive economy.[2]

The title of Ben Way's book, *Jobocalypse*, plays on the apocalyptic theme to present a much more limited sense of impending change. He asks if your job is in danger of getting replaced by robots and then looks at the rapidly changing face of robotics and how it will revolutionize employment and jobs over the next thirty years.[3]

The apocalyptic theme is not specifically approached in environmentalist Lester R. Brown's book, *Plan B: Rescuing a Planet under Stress and a Civilization in Trouble,*[4] but the impact is the same. When the Public Broadcasting Service produced a documentary based on the book, Scott Thill called *Plan B: Mobilizing to Save Civilization*[5] "likely the scariest horror film that was ever disguised as a documentary."

> That's because the acclaimed environmentalist has deeply studied the variety of environmental and geopolitical tipping points we are fast approaching, and found that we're headed for a seriously dark dystopia if we don't turn civilization as we know it around, and fast. A catastrophic confluence of food and water shortages, overpopulation and pollution, collapsed governments and communities and more natural disasters than Roland Emmerich can dream up await us on

the other side of Plan A, which Brown calls "business as usual."[6]

In 2010 James Carroll wrote a *Boston Globe* column called "Teetering on the Apocalypse" in which he pointed out the mythical elements underlying the threat of nuclear war in the Mideast. He concluded the column saying,

> That malign meta-historical forces were unleashed by the splitting of the atom is evident in the United States, where the nuclear arsenal spawned a subliminally religious militarism based on the creed that saving the world may actually require its destruction. Mutual assured destruction, in the mantra of deterrence theory. Better dead than Red, in the Cold War motto. Death as end game. So far, deterrence has worked at the global level, with the threat of nuclear Armageddon successfully keeping the superpower peace, but the cost of this hair-trigger nihilism to humankind's moral imagination has yet to be calculated.

> The apocalyptic mind is alive and well-armed and dangerous. If the Israelis and Palestinians succeed in defusing their local conflict, they will also have nudged the entire human family back from an impulse that, though long regarded as holy, is profoundly wicked. The earth was not created to end in a cataclysm of violence, and neither were Israel or Palestine. Peace, therefore. Shalom. Salaam.[7]

Barbara Ehrenreich was awarded an honorary degree on May 20, 2007 by Haverford College. Her commencement speech was challenging and she ended this way:

> And let me mention the most terrifying feature of the world you are entering: Ever notice how many movies, novels and TV series today are about a post-apocalyptic world? I'm thinking of everything from Cormac McCarthy's Pulitzer Prize-winning novel *The Road* to the new movie *28 Weeks Later*. Well, there's a reason for that: Our planet may be becoming less and less inhabitable, at least in any civilized way. And the change will be painfully evident within your lifetimes.

One thing that's for sure: Our way of life—our gas-guzzling, tree-destroying, extinction-producing way of life—is finished. We have to find a new way of life, and that's going to be your task. But if I have my say in it, it'll be one that involves having more fun, while using a lot less stuff.

Look, I'm really sorry about the mess my generation and your parents' generation is leaving to you: the cruel economy, the bloody quagmire of US foreign and military policy, our threatened habitat. And I just want you to understand that we tried to do better—maybe not enough of us, maybe not hard enough—but we tried. And now you have to try, only with one big difference. For us it was matter of idealism, for you it's a matter of survival. So, my final instruction to the class of '07: Go out there and raise hell![8]

In the June 4, 2013 posting of AlterNet, Don Hazen, its executive editor, wrote a column identifying what he called the four plagues or four horsemen of our time. They are, he says, analogous to the four horsemen of the Revelation of St. John. When the Lamb of God, or Lion of Judah (Jesus Christ) opens the first four of the seven seals, four beings ride out on white, red, black, and pale horses. The four riders symbolize Conquest, War, Famine, and Death.

Hazen's contemporary four horsemen are privatization, financialization, militarization, and criminalization, "which together are producing a steadily creeping authoritarianism—a new authoritarianism—to fit our times." Hazen attributes the identification of the first three plagues to Cornell West for whom they were examples of what he sees as our society heading toward fascism.[9]

- Financialization is the big banks and investment entities making money by simply moving money around or quite openly stealing it from their "customers."

- Privatization is the process of maneuvering community assets like prisons, schools, and roads from public ownership to for-profit corporations.

- Militarization is equipping the INS, ATF, FBI, DEA, and local police forces with drones, armored vehicles, and SWAT team weaponry and armor (if you have SWAT teams the impulse is to use them). Funding the Pentagon dominates the federal budget and supports military bases in 63 countries around the world and all across the U.S. as well. The United States is the world's largest arms dealer.

- Criminalization turns whole populations—immigrants, blacks, Latinos—into hoods for things like being such or possessing minute amounts of marijuana. Nearly 90% of those stopped in the Stop and Frisk police program in NYC are black or Latino.

The four horsemen are representatives of the powerful dominators: the predatory capitalists and their retainers in the three branches of our government.

What are the common folks up to while the 1% predatory capitalist dominators are ripping us off and living large in their gated communities and sunbathing on their beautiful yachts?[10]

That's our next episode.

---

[1] David Denby, "Life and Undeath," *The New Yorker,* July 1, 2013, a review of *WWZ.*

[2] Robert Jensen, *We Are All Apocalyptic Now: On the Responsibilities of Teaching, Preaching, Reporting, Writing, and Speaking Out,* in print at Amazon.com and on Kindle (CreateSpace Independent Publishing Platform, 2013).

[3] Ben Way, *Jobocalypse: The End of Human Jobs and How Robots Will Replace Them,* CreateSpace Independent Publishing Platform (June 21, 2013).

[4] W. W. Norton & Company, 1st edition (October 17, 2003). Brown has published three revisions, the last being *Plan B 4.0: Mobilizing to Save Civilization.*

[5] *Plan B: Mobilizing to Save Civilization* focuses on the growing threat of global warming while also providing viewers with a roadmap to develop ways to mitigate and adapt to these emerging challenges. Featured are environmental visionary Lester Brown, Nobel laureate Paul Krugman, Tom Friedman, former Secretary of the Interior Bruce Babbitt, and other leading scientists and policymakers.

[6] AlterNet, posted on March 26, 2011. http://www.alternet.org/story/150385/

[7] James Carroll, "Teetering on the Apocalypse," *The Boston Globe,* September 20, 2010. http://jaldenh.wordpress.com/2010/09/20/teetering-on-the-apocalypse-by-james-carroll/

[8] Barbara Ehrenreich, "The Apocalypse is Yours Now," Huffington Post, May 21, 2007. www.huffingtonpost.com/.../the-apocalypse-is-yours-n_b_48988.html

[9] http://www.alternet.org/economy/4-plagues-getting-handle-coming-apocalypse?

[10] NationofChange at: http://www.nationofchange.org/we-re-all-being-poisoned-deregulated-capitalism-1376234335

Chapter 5

Manifold reactions to the apocalypse of civilization

IN ONE WAY OR ANOTHER almost all of us are aware that civilization is terminally diseased and that the apocalypse is ever more apparent. The nature of our awareness and how we respond to it is largely determined by our place in the social structure and our psychological makeup.

We are like cancer patients. While most of us are blessed with systems that reject cancerous cells, others of us have small active tumors but have no idea that we are in peril. Though diseased, we continue to live in a surreal trance. Some of the folks in a trance are terminally stupid. They seem to be numbed by blissful ignorance. Those who suffer from mental illness are exempt, of course, from such classifications and need our persistent loving care and acceptance.

There are those who behave as one might at an early stage of any terminal disease. They are discomfited, but haven't made any diagnostic guesses. They may be trapped in social and cultural backwaters, isolated from the wider world. Others may have been, for circumstances not of their own making, discarded by society as worthless or worse. And, finally, there are some among us who are, by necessity, totally absorbed in survival strategies. Hanging on by a fingernail, they are at the very bottom of Abraham Maslow's Need Hierarchy.[1]

Many of us, however, are well aware of the pain caused by the cancerous tumor in the belly of our culture, and realize we are in a terminal state. We are awake, taking nourishment, and conscious of the causes of our disease; we are in pain about the ongoing loss of things that made life rich in the imaginary good old days. Even those who are still protected from the immediate impact of environmental degradation, income disparity, and predatory capitalist rapacity, and who are not feeling much pain, may nevertheless have a gut feeling that our civilization is threatened and wasting away.

How are people in America reacting to the impending death of civilization?

As a way of categorizing the variety of the symptomatic (psychological and social) responses to the fatal disease of the domination system, I have found it helpful to look at it through a now-classic framework that Dr. Elisabeth Kübler-Ross developed for understanding the grief process in terminal patients. She identified five emotional stages that patients went through as they were dying: denial, anger, bargaining, depression, and acceptance.[2]

While Kübler-Ross originally applied these stages of the grief process to people suffering from terminal illness, she later expanded her model to include any form of catastrophic personal loss. Such losses can include many significant life events: the death of a loved one, a major rejection, end of a relationship or divorce, the onset of a disease or chronic illness, as well as natural disasters like fires, floods, earthquakes, and tornados. The grief process is also stimulated in the survivors of human-style murder and mayhem.

It is a mistake to think that the grief process moves in a linear fashion from one stage to another. The process is more complex than that. A person may move, for example, directly from denial to bargaining and then back to feeling deeply angry when the bargain is not struck. Others may move very quickly to acceptance and seemingly not experience denial or anger or bargaining. Further, the process may recycle two or three times, and some folks never make it to the stage of acceptance; following the patterns of domination-of-violence systems, they continue to fight to the very end.

Since we are talking about an apocalyptic process, a terminal illness that has impacted most of the people on the planet, let's look at how different groups are dealing with our dying civilization.

I. <u>Denial</u>—Who are the folks in denial or oblivion?

The predatory capitalist, 1% oligarchs are either in denial, or are engaged in keeping their fears under control while they pile up assets designed to protect themselves from death as long as possible.

The ruling class and the faithful retainers to the oligarchs are in denial. They are loyal and committed to serving their masters under the illusion that they will be protected and carried along to the end. They are convinced that they will ultimately find their release from the symptoms of the deadly disease. They are the politicians, public servants, money movers, and bureaucrats who keep the business-as-usual show running and profitable for their bosses. The producers of mass media and conservative clergy are among their numbers. Many of the retainer class people are 10%-ers.

As noted earlier, there are whole cadres of people who are captive to the domination system mindset and cling to the myth that success and wealth are possible for them. For now they see themselves as simply going through a rough patch. In the meantime they anesthetize themselves from the pain of the disease by focusing on sports and reality television, thereby saturating themselves in the consumerist propaganda called advertising.

The fundamentalist religious devotees of all faiths who continue to believe in the creation myths and fictions of their earliest documents are also in denial. They admit to none of the wisdom that evolved for humankind during the Age of Enlightenment. They steadfastly denounce or systematically ignore the wisdom of the sciences. A very small number of flat-earthers are included in this group. They haven't had a clue about much of anything for centuries.

There are a small number of *millennialists* in denial of sorts. They are convinced that the end is near, indeed are rejoicing over this very thing. They are waiting to be raised into heaven when the Rapture arrives, which is certain to happen on the date next announced by the most deluded prophet and certainly before the next millennium.

II. <u>Anger</u>—Who are the angry and violent ones?

Tea Party members and followers; most of them are white middle class folks angry at being unemployed, manipulated, and marginalized. They see themselves as victims who are denied the benefits that they perceive to be provided to most others. Interestingly, they see blacks, Hispanics, and Muslims, many of whom are actually worse off than themselves, as being privileged.

There are, however, several different manifestations of the Tea Party.

First, there is a slowly eroding consortium of local groups of relatively innocent folks who participate in small demonstrations and local actions to protest their plight. In another manifestation are political operatives who have co-opted the energy of the disenchanted regular folks in the Tea Party and have turned the Party into a tool of the oligarchs.

Second, there are overtly political takeovers of the popular unrest.

The *Congressional Tea Party Caucus* was founded by Representative Michelle Bachman. Grassroots members received it with mixed emotions.[3].

The *Tea Party Express* was organized by a political consulting firm in Los Angeles. The Express collects and distributes contributions to selected political candidates.

The *Tea Party Patriots* are a confusing segment of the Party. They are well organized and claim to be a genuine grassroots movement. While denying it, they have been accused of receiving financial and organizational help from Freedom Works, a clearly political group, which was once headed by former House Majority leader Dick Armey.[4]

The *Sovereign Citizens Movement*,[5] a more troublesome group of angry people, had its origins in the 1970s when far right-wingers formed a loose association called the *Posse Comitatus*. They believed that the County was the largest legitimate government and took steps to dissociate themselves from state and federal law.

A significant step in the growth of the *Sovereign Citizens Movement* occurred in August of 1992 when federal marshals and the FBI surrounded the home of separatist Randy Weaver and his family in Ruby Ridge, Idaho and took siege. Eleven days later, after a chaotic attack on the family compound, the Weavers' ward, a 14-year-old boy, Randy's 42-year-old wife, a federal marshal, and a yellow Labrador retriever had been shot dead. The full story of the siege is a terrible indictment of the US marshals and the FBI.[6]

Another government terrorist operation further helped to generate the passion that characterizes the *Sovereign Citizens Movement*. In 1993 the FBI attacked the Mount Carmel Center, the home of David Koresh's Branch Davidian community in Elk, Texas, nine miles from Waco. The Branch Davidians believed a prophecy that there was an imminent apocalypse with the second coming of Jesus Christ and the defeat of evil armies of Babylon. According to Koresh, God told him to start building an "Army for God" to prepare for the end of days and salvation for his followers. The attack ended when fire engulfed the Mount Carmel Center and 76 men, women, and children, including David Koresh, died.[7]

The *Militia Movement* arises from the notion that armed militia groups are sanctioned by the Constitution but does not subordinate them to the federal government. Members of the movement believe that militias were designed to oppose and, if necessary, overthrow governments that become tyrannical. Some members believe that behind the federal government's alleged slide toward tyranny is a globalist conspiracy they identify as the "New World Order." The movement's ideology has led some committed members to commit crimes which have included include stockpiling illegal weapons and explosives, plotting to destroy government buildings, and assassinate public officials, as well as lesser confrontations.[8]

One *Militia Movement* plot to destroy government buildings was brought to its conclusion on the second anniversary of the attack on the Branch Davidians. Early on the afternoon of April 19, 1995, an enormous explosion ripped off the front of the Murrah Federal Building in Oklahoma City.

Timothy McVeigh and Terry Nichols made a huge bomb in the back of a truck that McVeigh parked outside the Murrah Federal Building. He left it and then detonated it, killing 168 people and injuring 680 more. The bombing destroyed or damaged 324 buildings and shattered glass in 285 others, resulting in damages estimated at $652 million.

McVeigh and Nichols were firmly committed anti-government rhetoricians and had been since serving in the Army together. In the year before the Oklahoma bombing, McVeigh's anti-government rhetoric escalated. He was making his living at gun shows where he distributed videos and handed out pamphlets with titles like "U.S. Government Initiates Open Warfare Against American People" and "Waco Shootout Evokes Memory of Warsaw '43." It was the Waco assault that pushed him over the edge to seek vengeance on the federal government.

The *Militia Movement* continues today, and the number of its adherents increased during the Great (or Global) Recession as distressed people reacted negatively to the election of President Obama. Wikipedia lists 81 militia organizations across the USA.

Finally, there is the *American Resistance Movement* (ARM). The Movement claims that American citizens of every race, religion, gender, nationality, and political affiliation are members of ARM. They are encouraged to monitor "all covert, secret and subversive government/military activity which might compromise America's National Security, The United States Constitution, and agencies like the DHS, TSA, CIA, NSA, BATF, and the DOD." They then may make all information available to the general public through national and independent news outlets. "ARM activities include research, reconnaissance, communication, activism, survival training, weapons training, preparation, humanitarian work, and nature conservation."[9]

Others who are caught in the grip of anger in reaction to the sense of apocalyptic collapse are . . .

. . . A wide variety of regressive historically challenged anti-socialists and anti-fascists who verge on anarchism and so tend to find organizations uncomfortable.

. . . Racists who believe that blacks and Hispanics are destroying America.

. . . The strident segment of members of the National Rifle Association who hold views similar to the members of the *Militia Movement* and the *Sovereign Citizens Movement*.

. . . Some elements within national, state, and local police forces who have been militarized and seduced into the role of protectors of the rights and rules of the predatory capitalists.

. . . Some voices and organizations in mass media that love to play on the fears and anger of the disaffected.

When frustrated and seemingly powerless, the angry ones can slide into violence or significant loss and hopelessness. Some of the more passive angry ones express their feelings in letters to the editor, tweets, Facebook posts, yard signs, and demonstrations calling for justice or righteousness.

III. Bargaining—Who are the bargainers?

The *Green Tea Party*[10] seeks to be a more conciliatory and collaborative organization that brings people of diverse political and social viewpoints together in an effort to find mutually acceptable solutions to common problems. Their motto is *"Making a More Perfect Union—One Cup at a Time!"*

Active and passive members of political parties are bargainers who are not themselves members of the ruling or retainer class. They suffer under the impression that if they can garner enough votes and supporters they can make significant moves to counteract the entrenched dominating power of the greedy and aggrandizing predatory capitalists.

A large number of bargainers belong to nonprofit, activist, and educational organizations like the League of Conservation Voters, Common Cause, The Nature Conservancy, The Sierra Club, The Friends National Committee on Legislation, People for the American Way, and many other such interest groups.

IV. <u>Depression</u>—Who are the depressed?

When Dr. Kübler-Ross used the term depression to describe the fourth stage of the grief process, I don't think she meant clinical depression as it is defined by the psychiatric profession. It is clear that people coping with impending death or significant loss may experience symptoms of situational depression. Their symptoms include feeling sad or empty, feeling hopeless, feeling very tired, and perhaps thinking about suicide.

If you have ever had a bout with depression, you know well what it does to you. I remember the days of depression I suffered when my first marriage was in its dying days. I didn't want to get out of bed. I had work to do, but I couldn't get at it. I didn't want to hang out with my kids. I was in a kind of stupor. My depression broke when a recollection from Wilson Van Dusen's book, *Natural Depth in Man,* struck me as "Do something! Anything." I went downstairs to my rudimentary workshop and nailed together a cubist-like sculpture of scrap lumber. Then about two hours after I made it, I went back down and smashed it to pieces. That broke the spell of my depression.

The people who are depressed as a result of the massive changes arising as a result of the apocalypse of civilization are mostly suffering from powerlessness and a total lack of hope. They no longer feel or think that there is any possibility for them to live well and thrive. In essence they have given up on the system and so have given up on themselves. Depression is not a self-inflicted condition.

Most of the folks who are depressed simply drop out of sight. They are the ones who live in cheap hotels, homeless camps, on the streets, and in deteriorating houses. They are the elderly and obsoleted people who live in the dying small towns and run-down neighborhoods scattered throughout the country in both red and blue states. They are the parents of the 22% of children living in poverty. They are stoners and meth addicts. They are at the bottom of the social hierarchy and are too often regarded as expendables. They are called lazy, good-for-nothing freeloaders, and the objects of the predatory capitalist/elite/conservative campaign to eliminate them.

V. Acceptance—Who are the acceptors?

That's for our next episode.

---

[1] Abraham H. Maslow, "A Theory of Human Motivation" [Kindle Edition], www.all-about-psychology.com

[2] Elisabeth Kübler-Ross, *On Death and Dying: What the Dying Have to Teach Doctors, Nurses, Clergy, and Their Own Families,* Scribner Classics, 1997.

[3] Kenneth P. Vogel, "Tea Party vs. Tea Party Caucus," POLITICO, Tea Party movement, Aug 2, 2010. http://www.politico.com/news/stories/0810/40528.html

[4] Eric Lach, "More Details Emerge About Dick Armey's Failed FreedomWorks Coup," TPM Muckraker, June 27, 2013. http://talkingpointsmemo.com/muckraker/more-details-emerge-about-dick-armey-s-failed-freedomworks-coup

[5] http://en.wikipedia.org/wiki/Sovereign_citizen_movement

[6] http://www.trutv.com/library/crime/gangsters_outlaws/cops_others/randy_weaver/2.html

[7] http://en.wikipedia.org/wiki/Waco_siege

[8] http://en.wikipedia.org/wiki/Militia_movement

[9] http://americanresistancemovement.ning.com

[10] http://www.greenteaparty.us

Chapter 6

Accepting the apocalypse of civilization

BEFORE GOING ANY FURTHER with an attempt to identify those who are accepting the signs of civilization's impending death, we look back at what Dr. Elisabeth Kübler-Ross meant about the process of accepting death. The acceptance stage of the grief process begins with words like, "That's it. It's over. What will be will be, and there's nothing I can do about it now. Let's make the best of it," and similar phrases. Acceptance is the tacit or expressed acknowledgement that death will happen on a not-too-distant day and that it is now appropriate to organize life between now and the end.

How the process is managed will depend on the circumstances that bring it about. When a disease has turned deadly, it is often very difficult for an infirm and debilitated person to manage the process without the help of a very supportive circle of loved ones. For others who are nearly fully functional, the acceptance of impending death may mean acquiescence and submission, withdrawal, quiet resignation, or a retreat back into a terminal depression.

Sadly, I know old friends in relatively good health who are convinced that the jig is up for life as they have known and remember it. They have given up doing anything but keeping on and keeping up the old ways as they wait to die and are hoping to do so before their children suffer while attempting to survive in a post-civilized world.

Even more sadly, we must grieve for people like the traditional farmers in India, who are committing suicide in epidemic numbers as they see their way of life destroyed by corporate Big Ag.

When death is imminent, yet somewhat distant, and there is a window of vitality, it may be possible to identify and, perhaps, choose a new frame of reference. In such circumstances one can identify a new way of looking at things that involves letting go of old ways of thinking and adopting new patterns of living out one's days. Blessed are those who, while dying, are yet strong enough to do what we do every day of our lives as we deal with changes that happen to us through the vicissitudes of ordinary daily existence. The process means creating a new pattern of life that focuses on the power of love to build new ways of living and being—as from a pattern of lifelong victimhood to a final period of audacious courage.

At this juncture, let us focus on those who are strong, still in good health, who accept the revelation that civilization is dying, and who are trying to figure out how to reshape our existence to survive through its death and create a new post-civilized human being.

There are two somewhat different themes operating among those who are ready to deal with the death of civilization: one, an environmental theme and the other, a socio-cultural theme. The environmentalists focus on the threat posed by global warming and its impact on the environment and the world's populations. The sociologists focus more on the collapse of the social structure of civilization. These two themes are, of course, arbitrary designations and don't adequately acknowledge the complexity of the relationship between environmental degradation, the diminishing quality of life for most people, and the overreaching aggrandizement of the capitalist ruling oligarchs and their economy.

The most frightening symptom of the apocalypse of civilization is the increasing knowledge that global warming will almost certainly result in the extinction of many species and vast numbers of, if not all, humans. Global warming is a direct result of the overreach of industrialization fueled by capitalism. The military-industrial complex and the fossil fuel industry primarily cause environmental and cultural degradation. Those mechanisms serve the oligarchs in pursuit of worldwide domination to further their avaricious acquisition and exploitation of coal, oil, and gas resources as they orchestrate the increased (ab)use of fossil fuel-based energy.

The Nobel prizewinning economist Paul Krugman, in a review of William D. Nordhaus's new book in the *New York Review of Books*,[1] has clearly delineated the relationship between industrialization and global warming.

> . . . we have been living in an age of unusual climate stability . . . "the last 7,000 years have been the most stable climatic period in more than 100,000 years." As Nordhaus notes, this era of stability coincides pretty much exactly with the rise of civilization, and that probably isn't an accident.
>
> Now that period of stability is ending—and civilization did it, via the Industrial Revolution and the attendant mass burning of coal and other fossil fuels. Industrialization has, of course, made us immensely more powerful, and more flexible too, more able to adapt to changing circumstances. The Scientific Revolution that accompanied the revolution in industry has also given us far more knowledge about the world, including an understanding of what we ourselves are doing to the environment.
>
> But it seems that we have, without knowing it, made an immensely dangerous bet: namely, that we'll be able to use

the power and knowledge we've gained in the past couple of centuries to cope with the climate risks we've unleashed over the same period. Will we win that bet? Time will tell. Unfortunately, if the bet goes bad, we won't get another chance to play.

The September 2013 report from the Intergovernmental Panel on Climate Change (IPCC) is unequivocal: Carbon dioxide in the atmosphere is responsible for a dramatic and escalating increase in earth and ocean temperatures.[2] Thom Hartmann, writing on that report in his article "Almost Too Horrible to Contemplate: Global Warming Could Destroy the Lives of 750 Million People in the Short Future,"[3] has this to say.

And that's how many people [750 million —Ed.], within the next 22 years, will almost certainly run low on water—a necessity of life—in just the regions whose rivers are supplied with water from the glaciers in the Himalayas.

To put that in perspective, 750 million people is more than twice the current population of United States. It's about the population of all of Europe. In the year 1900 there were only 500 million people on the entire planet. Seven hundred fifty million people is a lot of people.

The IPCC—the international body of scientists analyzing global climate change—is releasing its new report in stages over the next week and the *Financial Times* reported on this early piece on Monday[4]. Under the headline "Climate Change Chief Sounds Alert on Himalayan Glaciers," the opening sentence of the article by Pilita Clark summarizes it very tightly:

"The glaciers of the Himalayas are melting so fast they will affect the water supplies of a population twice that of the US within 22 years, the head of the world's leading authority on climate change has warned."

I have not been able to find the source of Thom Hartmann's figures. It may be that he has interpreted the high PPC report in the context of the data and estimations presented in his book, *The Last Hours of Humanity: Warming the World to Extinction.*[5] He has obviously accepted the conclusion that the threat of global warming means the death of civilization.

Let's identify some of the acceptors and take a brief look at what they have to say.

Rachel Carson

It would be disrespectful not to credit Rachel Carson as the primary predictor of the collapse and death of civilization. It was in 1962 that her book, *Silent Spring,* first rattled our cage.[6] The core of her argument was that pesticides (DDT being a prime example) were causing dramatic disastrous effects on the natural world and on human beings. Carson is widely recognized as a founder of the environmental movement, which has since become a force for reversing environmental degradation.

Bill McKibben

One of Carson's heirs, McKibben is said to be the first person to write a book for the general public on global warming. His book *The End of Nature*[7] was published in 1989, 27 years after Carson's clarion call. McKibben had hoped that his book would provoke action to reverse the process of global warming. Public inertia frustrated that hope. In 2010, after nearly a twenty-year gap, his book *Eaarth: Making a Life on a Tough New Planet* presents a much more pessimistic take on the subject.

> Here's all I'm trying to say: The planet on which our civilization evolved no longer exists. The stability that produced that civilization has vanished; epic changes have begun.
>
> We may, with commitment and luck, yet be able to maintain a planet that will sustain some kind of civilization, but it won't be the same planet, and hence it can't be the same

civilization. The earth that we knew—the only earth that we ever knew—is gone.[8]

It's true that by some measures we started too late, that the planet has changed and that it will change more.

The momentum of the heating, and the momentum of the economy that powers it, can't be turned off quickly enough to prevent hideous damage. But we will keep fighting, in the hope that we can limit that damage. And in the process, with many others fighting similar battles, we'll help build the architecture for the world that comes next, the dispersed and localized societies that can survive the damage we can no longer prevent. Eaarth represents the deepest of human failures. But we still must live on the world we've created—lightly, carefully, gracefully.[9]

Dmitry Orlov

Another pioneer in accepting the demise of civilization, Orlov was born in Russia and emigrated to the U.S. when he was twelve. As a young man he frequently traveled back to his native country and witnessed first-hand the collapse of the Soviet Union during the period leading up to 1991 and after. He used those experiences to develop a hypothesis about the process of collapse in the West. He first published his analysis in three articles in 2005 on "Post-Soviet Lessons for a Post-American Century" for From The Wilderness, a web project focused on peak oil.[10] His aim is to cut through vague talk about the end of civilization with a five-step prescription for the collapse in the West. He then expanded on that work in his book *Reinventing Collapse: The Soviet Example and American Prospects* in 2008. A *New Yorker* article in 2009 said of the book that "Orlov describes 'superpower collapse soup' common to both the U.S. and the Soviet Union: a severe shortfall in the production of crude oil, a worsening foreign-trade deficit, an oversized military budget, and crippling foreign debt."[11]

And then, in 2013, Orlov further elaborated on his thesis in *The Five Stages of Collapse*, which he identified as:

Stage 1: Financial collapse. Faith in "business as usual" is lost. The future is no longer assumed to resemble the past in any way that allows risk to be assessed and financial assets to be guaranteed. Financial institutions become insolvent; savings are wiped out and access to capital is lost.

Stage 2: Commercial collapse. Faith that "the market shall provide" is lost. Money is devalued and/or becomes scarce, commodities are hoarded, import and retail chains break down and widespread shortages of survival necessities become the norm.

Stage 3: Political collapse. Faith that "the government will take care of you" is lost. As official attempts to mitigate widespread loss of access to commercial sources of survival necessities fail to make a difference, the political establishment loses legitimacy and relevance.

Stage 4: Social collapse. Faith that "your people will take care of you" is lost, as local social institutions, be they charities or other groups that rush in to fill the power vacuum, run out of resources or fail through internal conflict.

Stage 5: Cultural collapse. Faith in the goodness of humanity is lost. People lose their capacity for "kindness, generosity, consideration, affection, honesty, hospitality, compassion, charity." Families disband and compete as individuals for scarce resources. The new motto becomes "May you die today so that I can die tomorrow."[12]

In an article appearing on his ClubOrlov blog in October of 2013, Orlov repented his optimism in *The Five Stages* book:

And so it seems that there may not be a happy end to my story of *The Five Stages of Collapse,* the first three of which (financial, commercial, political) are inevitable, while the last two (social, cultural) are entirely optional but have, alas, already run their course in many parts of the world. Because, you see, there is also the sixth stage which I have previously neglected to mention—environmental collapse—at the end of which we are left without a home, having rendered Earth (our home planet) uninhabitable.[13]

And who are some of the other acceptors?

Thom Hartmann is the author of *The Last Hours of Humanity: Warming the World to Extinction*, cited above.

Carolyn Baker, Ph.D. is the author of *SACRED DEMISE: Walking The Spiritual Path of Industrial Civilization's Collapse.* Her website Speaking Truth to Power has an excellent and comprehensive collection of articles and reviews on the collapse of industrial civilization.[14]

Dr. Brian Moench is the president of Utah Physicians for a Healthy Environment and a member of the Union of Concerned Scientists. He is the author of "Death by Corporation," an article in three parts that appeared on Truthout in June, July, and August of 2013.[15]

Mike Adams is the editor of *Natural News*, which published his article "14 signs that the collapse of our modern world has already begun," May, 2011. The signs he identifies are:

1 - Tornadoes, hurricanes, earthquakes, and tsunamis
2 - The silence of the bees
3 - The failure of nuclear science
4 - The vicious pursuit of Wikileaks
5 - The rise of the medical police state
6 - The increasing frequency of food shortages and crop failures
7 - The runaway destruction of the world by energy companies
8 - The continued GMO contamination of our planet
9 - The tyranny and criminal crackdowns targeting real food (raw milk)
10 - The escalation of the counterfeiting of the money supply
11 - The plummeting intelligence of the masses
12 - The complete and utter fabrication of the mainstream news

13 - The ongoing pharmaceutical pollution of our world

14 - The radioactive contamination of the global food supply

. . . make no mistake: We are already living in the collapse of our modern world. And you have a front-row seat! (Exciting, huh?) These are the End Times of the corporate oligarchy; the monopolistic for-profit corporation machine that destroyed everything in our world in exchange for a slightly higher quarterly earnings report.[16]

James Howard Kunstler is a prolific social critic, writer, and blogger (Clusterfuck Nation). On his blog page, the advertisement for his 2012 book, *Too Much Magic: Wishful Thinking, Technology, and the Fate of the Nation*[17] says,

The nationally best-selling author of *The Long Emergency*[18] expands on his alarming argument that our oil-addicted, technology-dependent society is on the brink of collapse— that the long emergency has already begun.

Robert Jensen is a professor in the School of Journalism at the University of Texas at Austin and author of a very short Kindle Edition book, *We Are All Apocalyptic Now: On the Responsibilities of Teaching, Preaching, Reporting, Writing, and Speaking Out.*[19]

The planet on which our civilization evolved no longer exists. The stability that produced that civilization has vanished; epic changes have begun. We may, with commitment and luck, yet be able to maintain a planet that will sustain some kind of civilization, but it won't be the same planet, and hence it won't be the same civilization. The earth that we knew—the only earth that we ever knew—is gone.[20]

To think apocalyptically is not to give up on ourselves, but only to give up on the arrogant stories we modern humans have been telling about ourselves. Our hope for a decent future—indeed, any hope for even the idea of a future— depends on our ability to tell stories not of how humans have ruled the world but how we can live in the world. The royal must give way to the prophetic and the apocalyptic. The central story of power—that the domination/subordination dynamic is natural and inevitable—must give way to stories of dignity, solidarity, and equality. We must resist not only the cruelty of repression but the seduction of comfort.

Naomi Klein is a relative newcomer to the ranks of the acceptors. As late a 2009 she was a denier. It might be fairer to say that she was on the fence. While she recognized there was a problem, she thought there were ways to avoid the cataclysm that is to come. By 2013, however, she was hard at work on a book that shows she is now an acceptor: *This Changes Everything: Capitalism vs. The Climate.*[21]

In a review article on occupy.com, Steve Rushton says Klein is now "a leading global thinker" who is hoping that a mass public movement will be inspired by countering capitalism by "Blockadia—a fluid and growing space of civil disobedience camps, blockades, sit-ins, lock-ons and other direct actions gaining worldwide attention against the extractive industries."[22]

Naomi Klein's change of heart and mind was telegraphed in an article in the *New Statesman* in October 2013 when she reported on the Fall Meeting of the American Geophysical Union in San Francisco. At the meeting much attention was given to a presentation by Brad Werner called "Is Earth F**ked? Dynamical Futility of Global Environmental Management and Possibilities for Sustainability via Direct Action Activism." Klein says,

> The bottom line (of Werner's talk) was clear enough: global capitalism has made the depletion of resources so rapid, convenient and barrier-free that "earth-human systems" are becoming dangerously unstable in response. When pressed by a journalist for a clear answer on the "are we f**ked" question, Werner set the jargon aside and replied, "More or less."

Werner is part of a small but increasingly influential group of scientists whose research into the destabilisation of natural systems—particularly the climate system—is leading them to similarly transformative, even revolutionary, conclusions. And for any closet revolutionary who has ever dreamed of overthrowing the present economic order in favour of one a little less likely to cause Italian pensioners to hang themselves in their homes, this work should be of particular interest. Because it makes the ditching of that cruel system in favour of something new (and perhaps, with lots of work, better) no longer a matter of mere ideological preference but rather one of species-wide existential necessity.[23]

As more and more people begin to accept the end of civilization and the possible extinction of life on our planet, we may have the possibility of a cultural revolution that can extend if not arrest the planetary degradation caused by our captivity in the domination/violence system. Klein holds out that hope even as she is pessimistic about it.

There are more acceptors every day. Are you ready to become an acceptor?

The gross extravagances of the dominating oligarchy, the predatory capitalists, and our capitulation to the myths of an ever-expanding economy have combined to bring us to the end point. The domination system, the social infrastructure that has shaped human life since 6000 BCE, is now at an end. We are living in the time of apocalypse, the death of civilization.

Are you ready to accept that the death of civilization means that you, too, will die? You may die as a result of one or another of the oncoming global environmental catastrophes, but more important right now, however, are these questions:

Are you ready to be an instrument for creating a brave new transitional culture that might evolve into a new, post-civilized humanity based on empathic love and mutuality, the alternative to domination and violence?

We're going to look at some of the groups and movements that are working on evolutionary alternatives to the death-dealing system.

That's what we're going to work on next.

---

[1] Paul Krugman, "Gambling with Civilization," *New York Review of Books,* November 7, 2013, a review of *The Climate Casino: Risk, Uncertainty, and Economics for a Warming World,* by William D. Nordhaus, Yale University Press 2013, 378 pp.

[2] The Intergovernmental Panel on Climate Change (IPCC) is the leading international body for the assessment of climate change. It was established by the United Nations Environment Programme (UNEP) and the World Meteorological Organization (WMO) in 1988 to provide the world with a clear scientific view on the current state of knowledge in climate change and its potential environmental and socio-economic impacts. In the same year, the UN General Assembly endorsed the action by WMO and UNEP in jointly establishing the IPCC. In March, 2014, the IPCC issued a 5th report available online at http://www.ipcc.ch/index.htm#.UzmzdNx5g0o.

[3] Thom Hartmann, Truthout, September 26, 2013. http://www.alternet.org/environment/global-warming-could-potentially-destroy-lives-750-million-people-next-three-decades

[4] September 21, 2013.

[5] Thom Hartmann, *The Last Hours of Humanity: Warming the World to Extinction,* Waterfront Digital Press, Kindle Edition.

[6] Rachel Carson, *Silent Spring,* Mariner Books, 2002 (first pub. Houghton Mifflin, 1962). ISBN 0-618-24906-0. *Silent Spring* initially appeared serialized in three parts in the June 16, June 23, and June 30, 1962 issues of *The New Yorker* magazine.

[7] Bill McKibben, *The End of Nature,* Random House Trade Paperbacks, 2006. A new edition of the 1989 publication.

[8] Bill McKibben, *Eaarth: Making a Life on a Tough New Planet* (Kindle Locations 523–528). Henry Holt and Co., Kindle Edition, 2010.

[9] Bill McKibben, *Eaarth: Making a Life on a Tough New Planet,* Henry Holt and Co., Kindle Edition, 2007, p. 211.

[10] From The Wilderness: Information on Peak Oil, Sustainability, www.fromthewilderness.com

[11] Ben McGrath, "The Dystopians," *The New Yorker,* January 26, 2009.

[12] Dmitry Orlov, *The Five Stages of Collapse,* New Society Publishers, 2013, p. 14.

[13] http://cluborlov.blogspot.com/2013/10/the-sixth-stage-of-collapse.

[14] Carolyn Baker, *Speaking Truth to Power,* http://carolynbaker.net, Sacred Demise: Walking The Spiritual Path of Industrial Civilization's Collapse, iUniverse, Inc., New York/Bloomington, 2009.

[15] Brian Moench, "Death by Corporation," Truthout, June 2013.

[16] Mike Adams, "14 signs that the collapse of our modern world has already begun," May 2, 2011, http://www.naturalnews.com

[17] James Howard Kunstler, *Too Much Magic: Wishful Thinking, Technology, and the Fate of the Nation,* Atlantic Monthly Press, 2012.

[18] James Howard Kunstler, *The Long Emergency: Surviving the End of Oil, Climate Change, and Other Converging Catastrophes of the Twenty-First Century,* Grove Press, 2006.

[19] Robert Jensen, *We Are All Apocalyptic Now: On the Responsibilities of Teaching, Preaching, Reporting, Writing, and Speaking Out,* Kindle, Amazon 2013, p. 20.

[20] Op. cit., p. 74.

[21] Naomi Klein, *This Changes Everything: Capitalism vs. The Climate,* Simon & Schuster, September 2014.

[22] Steve Rushton, "This Changes Everything: Naomi Klein Takes on Capitalism vs. the Climate," Occupy.com, Oct. 29, 2014.

[23] http://www.newstatesman.com/2013/10/science-says-revolt

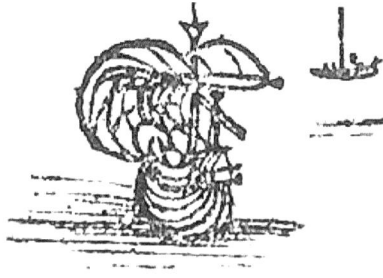

Part Two

Chapter 7

Why politics, revolutions, and some evolutions fail

In order to change an existing paradigm you do not struggle to try and change the problematic model. You create a new model and make the old one obsolete. That, in essence, is the higher service to which we are all being called.

—Buckminster Fuller

IN CHAPTERS 5 AND 6 we looked at the different responses to the imminent collapse of civilization in the categories developed by Elisabeth Kübler-Ross as she was working with people who were dying. I want to put aside for the moment the angry ones who are opting for a violent overthrow of the federal government or those who are suffering from situational depression, to focus on groups and movements that are working to find a way to cope with the collapse.

It is helpful to look back at the 1960s, when social change was a major theme in American culture. During that time there were any number of groups, organizations, and movements attempting to alter public policy in the direction of peace and justice. In an effort to understand what was going on in the New Left movements in the 1960s, Carl Boggs introduced the concept of prefigurative politics. Prefigurative politics applies to those groups and movements committed to social change and who attempt to live out relationships and political forms that "prefigure" the ideal society that they envisioned and were motivated to create.

Sociologist Wini Breines popularized the concept of prefigurative politics as it applied to New Left movements in the 1960s. She characterized the movements as "hostile to bureaucracy, hierarchy and leadership, and [they] took form as a revulsion against large-scale centralized and inhuman institutions." Breines clearly differentiated prefigurative action from strategic politics. Those who engage in strategic politics are "committed to building organizations in order to achieve power so that structural changes in the political, economic and social orders might be achieved."

The categories of strategic politics and prefigurative politics can be applied quite handily to the action groups and movements working to cope with the collapse of civilization. They can be divided into three broad categories: pure strategic organizations, hybrids that combine characteristics of both strategies, and prefigurative groups.

Category 1: Strategic organizations are organized as traditional social and political groups seeking to gain enough power to influence or modify the domination system to make it more just and more responsive to the variety of critical issues that comprise the threat of collapse.

Strategizers operate assuming that the domination system, the predatory capitalist oligarchical system, can be modified in ways that will avert or deflect its destructive inertia. They assume, for example, that ending the rape of the earth's resources will enable a recovery from ecological disaster. Their strategy can be stated this way: If we all band together into one large pressure group, or consortium of smaller pressure groups, we can reform the prevailing political and economic system. We can refashion its disastrous programs and turn it in a new direction. Let us organize to contend with the institutions that support the goals of the predatory capitalists. In other words, let's see if we can beat dominant oligarchs at their own game.

Category 2: Hybrid groups seek to amalgamate a wide variety of interests and concerns about the future into a unified nonviolent effort to undermine and/or overthrow the prevailing regime. Hybrid groups exhibit characteristics of both the strategic and prefigurative styles. Wini Breines analyzed this phenomenon in her work on social action groups in the 1960s. She discovered that the internal tension between the two options often eviscerates the effectiveness and outcomes of the work of hybrid groups.

Let's look at two hybrid movements in recent history: the Arab Spring and Occupy.

The Arab Spring is perhaps the closest we have come to a massive nonviolent resistance in recent history. What happened to the Arab Spring?

Before I attempt to answer that question, I need to talk about memes. Two phenomena operate to drive the process of evolution: the genome (the genetic material of an organism), and, for humans, memes. My sociologist son, Matthew Lawson, Ph.D., says this about memes:

> Genes are information units that direct development and interaction among system elements at the biological level. Memes are information units that direct development and interaction among system elements at the social/cultural level. These are different quantum levels. Genomes or "species" evolve to adapt to the wider physical/biological environment in which the species exists. "Coevolution" is key because a change in a genome can cause rippling

repercussions in the environment, forcing other genomes to adapt.

Cultures (memomes) evolve in similar ways, but with a crucial difference, which is that, since the neolithic revolution and the rise of civilization (citification) the human environment has been defined more by relations with other humans than by relations with the biological world. All the contemporary world religions arose in this stage of cultural evolution. All the world religions provide codes for action in complex human social environments and they provide effective rules for adaptation to these environments or they would have been selected against and died as memomes.[1]

Mimetic forces shape the process of change in human culture. Memes are more powerful than genes in determining what will happen in the future as we try to cope with climate change, collapse of the global economy, and the collapse of civilization itself.

If you are at all acquainted with the memes embedded in Egyptian culture over centuries, you probably made a very accurate prediction of what would happen to the country after the Arab Spring. You probably made the same accurate prediction about what would happen in Tunisia, and you were not surprised by the devastating confusion of conflicting resistance forces in Syria and Iraq.

Someone has famously said that a successful revolution always results in a regime worse than the one against which the people, or the military, revolted. That outcome is the product of a cluster of memes about leadership, governance, and government organization inherent in civilization. Those embedded memes demand that among the revolutionary forces there be a powerful, violent person or cadre with a disciplined array of retainers ready to enforce his or their dictates.

70

It is disturbing, but not surprising, to note that there are a number of cases where the imperialist goals of predatory capitalists propelled the United States government to undertake covert or overt military action to unseat or destroy popularly elected governments.[2] The outcome of those ventures is that the puppet regimes supported by the "victorious" Americans are worse than the ones undermined or destroyed. Even worse, the new regimes generate increased hostility to the United States. I simply note Chile, Iran, Iraq, Tunisia, Syria, and Afghanistan. At this writing the outcome of the United States' imperial warfare in the Mideast is yet to be determined. It may be a totally new configuration of nation-states and/or ongoing chaos for decades.

When reform of the existing system is an implicit or explicit goal of hybrid groups and movements, it is inevitable that their internal organization begins to tip in the direction of strategic politics, which is to say that they adopt the polity of civilization. In the absence of alternative memes that form and reinforce socially innovative prefigurative structures, what else do you expect? Idealism is a powerful motivator. If idealists want to effect real change, more than ideals are necessary. They must have a well-thought-out and disciplined program of action to follow both during and after the revolution. Idealists who want simply to overthrow the dominating powers are doomed to live in a worse regime.

Occupy was also a large and influential hybrid resistance movement. For a brief moment in our history the Occupy movement captured the imagination of folks aware that civilization is at an end and that new forms of human organization will be necessary to replace the dominance/violence hierarchical system we have inherited over thousands of years.

Two exciting prefigurative innovations in the early stages of the movement held out the promise of new patterns of human organization. Occupy sought to make decisions by consensus in the General Assembly, a large and very loosely structured crowd of variously motivated people. Occupy leaders cleverly innovated the People's Mic. They assumed these were ways of breaking out of the patterns of the hierarchical domination culture. The idealistic Occupy movement was, however, doomed from the beginning.

One major counterproductive factor undercut the promise of the Occupy movement. "Equality" memes, which emphasize that all people are equal and that all should have an equal voice, led to admitting dysfunctional street people and anarchists into the decision-making process and there was no way of managing those semi-psychotic manifestations. The General Assembly as a decision-making process became unwieldy because other than having the value (meme) of consensus-building, there was no disciplined structure to have serious deliberation in subgroups or in the larger group. Inevitably that led to decisions that had only minimal buy-in by the participants. The problem was discipline, or rather, the lack of discipline.

The beginning of the end of Occupy came through the oligarchs' retainers when, at the behest of the owner of Zuccotti Park, the New York City police department attacked and sacked the original Wall Street camp. When the Wall Street camp folded, so did the movement. Occupy camps across the country became targets of the oligarchs. Mainstream media stimulated political pressure. The retainer class in local governments went into action. Police and sheriff's departments, who have become both increasingly militarized and agents of the oligarchs, moved in on local camps on the basis of specious allegations that Occupy generated civil disruption. City by city, Occupy assemblies were shut down.

Sadly, the movement may have had exactly the opposite outcome than the one its creators projected in the beginning. The rise and fall of Occupy had the effect of causing the authorities to suppress of all kinds of legitimate public assemblies that were designed to expose the injustices of the domination system. Remnants of the Occupy movement quietly morphed into progressive hybrid groups. Occupy did not, however, morph into a typical domination hierarchical organization. The prefigurative progressive memes embedded in the Occupy ideal prevented that from happening.

It is my sense that people who are working under *the assumptions* of strategic politics may achieve some salutary results over the short haul, but are wasting much of their time and energy. I don't believe that a massive nonviolent resistance movement can be built. Even if it were built, I don't think it could overcome the enormous coercive and violent power that has been systematically aggregated by the oligarchy. Political strategy that confronts and challenges the domination system on its own grounds becomes just another way of underscoring and emphasizing its hegemony.

Category 3: Many prefigurative groups share a common aspiration. Rather than seeking ways to use political power to change the prevailing culture of the domination system to make it more just and equitable, they seek to establish small, largely local ventures experimenting with ways to live and thrive underground, apart from the structures of civilization. They say: We want to create new organizations and systems that can live outside the constraints of the systems and structures that are arrayed to maintain domination by the oligarchy. We will not attempt to change the domination system to be more equitable and just. We will let it die of its own inertia.

The majority of prefigurative groups are intentional communities—groups of people, individuals, families, and friends with common concerns and interests who gather together and make a commitment to organize their lives in new ways that are distinct from the traditional norms of civilized culture. There are many forms of intentional communities, from co-housing enterprises to almost-pure back-to-the-land communes.

The Fellowship for Intentional Community (FIC)[3] is a great resource for exploring intentional communities. Its international directory lists and describes the characteristics of 1665 intentional communities in the United States and many more around the world. FIC is a nonprofit dedicated to promoting cooperative culture. They say . . .

> We believe that intentional communities are pioneers in sustainable living, personal and cultural transformation, and peaceful social evolution. Intentional communities include *ecovillages, cohousing,* residential land trusts, income-sharing *communes,* student *co-ops,* spiritual communities, and other projects where people live together on the basis of explicit common values.

> Our passion is promoting cooperative culture and sustainable living. That means providing the information and inspiration for those seeking community, forming communities, struggling with the challenges of community, and those who want to develop a greater sense of community where they are.

Some of our pioneering neighbors are listed in the FIC directory.[4] I am acquainted with five of the intentional communities listed in Sonoma County, California and have learned something from friends about their internal dynamics. Three of them are cohousing developments: Yulupa Cohousing, which is 10 years old; Monan's Rill, and Santa Rosa Creek Commons, the last two started by Quakers in the 1970s. I also

74

know something about two pioneering communities that are clearly prefigurative in that they live an alternative lifestyle off the grid to some measure.[5] I would describe them as in, but not of, the dominant culture.

Each of the five communities is distinct from the dominant culture in that they do not operate by the usual rules of governance in the dominant culture. In making decisions about their life and work they do not debate, the do not vote, they do not use Robert's Rules of Order. They make decisions by consensus. Decisions at Monan's Rill follow a different pattern. They operate like Quakers, who seek to discern the deepest wisdom or the Spirit to enlighten their decisions, which they claim goes beyond consensus to unity.

All of the other communities operate in much the same way. Yulupa Cohousing, for example, has a number of committees that oversee various aspects of their community, from finances to maintenance to facilitating peaceable living. Each of the committees, operating by consensus, then brings its deliberations and decisions to monthly meetings of the whole community. This seems to be the pattern of governance in many intentional communities around the world and follows the example of the ZEGG Community[6] in Germany.

The domination/hierarchy/violence themes and memes of civilization pervade all traditional organizations from one-night stands to families, communities, businesses, universities, NPOs, and governments. Those themes and memes are built into our psyches, and when those factors creep into the life of prefigurative intentional communities they create conflict, win-lose scenarios, and bidding for power and control. Time and again, the communities with which I'm acquainted face these problems in trying to rule by consensus no matter how dedicated to the ideals of equity, peace, and nonviolence their members seem to be.

The memes around individualism create another hazard for intentional communities. Individualism as a value has become more and more prominent in the recent history of industrialized nations. Industrial production and organization require efficiency from reproducible units. Skillful individuals are highly valued. Families and other primary social units are bothersome things that impede profitability.[7] The primary value in an intentional community is that its members place the well-being of the community before their needs as individuals. When our civilized psyches infused with powerful individuality memes arise, they can seriously erode that primary commitment.

Intentional communities necessarily spend significant energy contending with the old, embedded civilization memes and reinforcing the new memes that motivated their creation and sustain their existence and continuing life.

Psychosis is another factor that can sabotage or undermine human organizations. We've seen how the equality memes of the Occupy movement, which considered all people as equals, undermined the effectiveness of their General Assemblies. In any system psychosis may not be evident in members until relationships are well aged and psychosis may manifest at virtually any stage of life. Psychosis in new and old members of a community may not be evident until they become disruptive. Psychotics tend not to do well in disciplined communities and, unfortunately, many communities do not develop the discipline to deal effectively with psychotics. Small intentional communities can be severely disrupted or become dysfunctional when one or two psychotics are members or guests.[8]

On those unhappy notes, in the next chapter we consider committing evolutionary suicide.

[1] Quotation from a personal email.

[2] Smedley D. Butler, *War is a Racket: The Antiwar Classic by America's Most Decorated Soldier*, Feral House, reprint edition, 2003. Originally printed in 1935, *War Is a Racket* is General Smedley Butler's frank speech describing his role as a soldier as nothing more than serving as a puppet for big-business interests.

[3] http://www.ic.org. I urge you to explore this website.

[4] http://www.ic.org.

[5] Some of the male members work for wages at enterprises in nearby cities and towns.

[6] ZEGG is an intentional community and an international conference center developing and implementing practical models for a socially and ecologically sustainable way of living. It is located southwest of Berlin and its full German name translates as the "Center for Experimental Culture Design." ZEGG was founded in 1991. http://www.zegg.de/en/

[7] When robots on an assembly line do most of the work even individuals become bothersome.

[8] Zeese & Flowers

http://www.alternet.org/visions/humanitys-crisis-systemic-and-overwhelming-and-only-way-out-create-bold-new-systems?akid=11514.77482.QqY64G&rd=1&src=newsletter959266&t=17

Chapter 8

Liberation begins in your belly, or, as we once called it, your soul

The world is so exquisite, with so much love and moral depth, that there is no reason to deceive ourselves with pretty stories for which there's little good evidence.

Far better, it seems to me, in our vulnerability, is to look Death in the eye and to be grateful every day for the brief but magnificent opportunity that life provides.

—*Carl Sagan*

SO FAR WE HAVE documented significant evidence that the social structure we call civilization is collapsing. Its collapse may be a good thing because the domination system will die with it. Surviving humans, having been liberated from violence and hierarchy, may be able to create a new post-civilized social order that might arise after the 6th Extinction.[1]

If our children, our grandchildren, and we are going to be among the surviving humans and be the creators of a new humanity, we will have to work at our liberation from the domination system prison and all its manifestations in our culture. If you look back to that earlier chapter in which I described the hierarchical structure of civilization, you remember that the Emperor's retainers are promised some of the

79

gifts, the power, status, and wealth that he holds. The covenant that the Emperor makes with his people is that they be obedient and follow his commands and directions in exchange for his assurance that they will maintain their security, their status, their wealth, and their power, or at least their hopes for such. The people, particularly those of the lower classes, are trapped by the violence of the Emperor on the one hand and on the other hand by their need to keep what minimal security they might be granted.

If you look at it closely, the same covenant exists between the people of the USA and its dominating oligarchy. The major themes of the American dream, Security, Status, Wealth, and Power, are designed to both imitate and emulate the imperial oligarchs.

Remember the description of memes in Chapter 7? Memes are information units that direct development and interaction among system elements at the social/cultural level. Since the Neolithic revolution and the rise of cities, the (memomes of) civilized cultures have defined relations with other humans more than by relations with the biological world.

The power of the systemic organizational structure of civilization continues because the culture (memome) of civilization is built into our psyche, our brains, and our consciousness. The memes (the concepts, patterns, symbols, myths, and images) of the last 8,000 years forcefully operate in our psyches, our souls, behind our awareness. They shape everything we think and do. They give form and pattern to our ideas and our relationships, of how we perceive reality. The culture of civilization is built into all the structures and systems in which we live: our families, civic organizations and nonprofits, our churches and communities as well as our states and nations. Our participation in all of these systems, shaped by domination and violence, serves to reinforce and strengthen the culture embedded in our psyches and vice versa.

Our first task is to deal with our souls and minds. As we get into that, however, we will begin to recognize that in so doing we are also dealing with the structures of our culture.

* * * * * * * * * * * * * * * * * * * *

As one looks at the predominant themes in the American dream as it is playing out in the 21st century, it becomes clear that the need for security is the most dominant need in our society today, and the amplification of fear, especially the fear of terrorism, is paramount in the attention of mainstream media. The tragedy of the deaths of less than 3000 people at the World Trade Center in 2001 is minute when compared to the number of fatalities on the highways of America, or the number of murders, suicides, and accidental deaths in a proliferating gun culture. The fear of terrorist attacks aroused in the population after 911 is, however, enormous compared to the more mundane fears of daily life on the streets and in the homes of America.

Security may come first and status may come second in our hopes and dreams. The fantasy that hard work will get you to any goal you want to reach is another theme that is sounded again and again. We hear that axiom voiced by young athletes, successful entrepreneurs, Ivy League geniuses, and, ironically, Donald Trump. The truth is that many other factors play into successful professional achievement, artistic success, or high status in any field of endeavor. Dumb luck is probably of greater significance than intense willpower and dedicated practice.

Along with security and status, the American dream includes such wealth as to be able to have a premium car or two, and a mega-mansion with a pool, hardwood floors, granite countertops, and stainless steel top-of-the line appliances in a gated community. It may also include enough money and leisure to take annual vacations abroad or, at least, to Disneyland.

Finally, the American dream holds out the hope of enough personal and in-group power, which means the ability to control one's life and the lives of others so that no ill may come to me, to mine, or to my extended family and friends. It is highly desirable to emulate the oligarchy in its ability to order life so as to overcome any adversity. Nowhere is this more visible than in the proliferation of end-game medical procedures to avert death.

We are trapped in the domination/violence system, the main component of civilization, by the hopes and aspirations that arise out of our desire to emulate the oligarchs. We are also trapped by an awareness of our vulnerability: the unspoken interior knowledge that we actually hang on by the skin of our teeth. Although we see all around us evidence of poverty, homelessness, dread disease, and the untimely deaths of our young neighbors, we are masters of the practice of denial.

The domination system and civilization are truly a response to the human fear of death. If you can get enough power, wealth, status, and security, you can grasp the illusion of immortality more closely and fend off the demons of death.

Before moving on there are a couple of things we need to get clear about. The first is both simple and yet very complex. The universe in which we find ourselves is a complete system, every part of which is connected to every other part with a complexity that science is only beginning, barely beginning, to understand.[2] The universe is a holism.

Second, the universe as we know it is a creation of our consciousness; its shape, its forces, its nature, its relationships are all functions of how we perceive it. Because our perceptions are shaped and informed by our intellectual/conceptual history, we see what we have been conditioned to see and we relate to the reality that has shaped our consciousness.

My friend Harry T. Cook[3] wrote about the time when, as he says, "I was griping about what I consider to be made-up words that appear in no dictionary. Not so much as turning her head whilst chopping vegetables, my wife Susan said: 'Everything after "oogah oogah" is made up,' referring to primitive *Homo sapiens*."[4]

Language is made up of the names we put on the stuff we appropriate with our senses. Sentences are how we structure the relationships of that stuff: subject, verb, and predicate. The words and sentences are not the same as the actuality of what we have named and related. Some time ago Alan Watts famously said, "The map is not the territory." We have to get it in our heads that we create reality and that we can and must continually re-create it.[5]

Civilization is a state of mind, an elaborate conceptual fiction. Looking at the history of our relationship to the universe, we can see major crises that reshaped our reality and, consequently, the structure of human society. Remember how Galileo's telescope enabled him to see something new.[6] Remember how he interpreted what he saw and how that changed the course of human history. Very slowly a new meme replaced an old one; man once was the center of the universe and is no longer.

Long ago humans constructed civilization with all its benefits and costs and now we must let it die and start over. Our liberation from the domination system and civilization is only possible if we do what seems to be totally contradictory, commit evolutionary suicide. We have to overcome our fear of dying in order to survive.

Lynice Pinkard is a progressive theologian and pastor in Oakland, California and one of the founders of the Seminary of the Street.[7] She has written about revolutionary suicide as a way of liberation for her friends and she has organized small groups using a modified 12-step process to help its members to die to the memes that have trapped them and beaten down their power to change themselves and the culture that has imprisoned them.[8]

Pinkard's model has helped me toward understanding that our personal pathway toward liberation from civilization consciousness is evolutionary suicide, a self-directed *metanoia*. In the Christian spiritual tradition, metanoia refers to a change that begins with penitence and leads to conversion, to a new orientation to life, to a new person free from the living perdition of original sin. In psychology, however, metanoia refers to the experience of a psychotic break and a subsequent healing, a positive psychological re-construction. Our psychological and spiritual task includes both forms of metanoia.[9]

Metanoia, as I am using the term, is not simply a change of mind. It is a planned psycho-spiritual breakdown followed by a studied reconstruction of one's consciousness; building a new way of understanding and acting. It is no less than the death of an old and the birth of a new you. Metanoia is a version of the process Huey Newton introduced in his autobiography *Revolutionary Suicide*.[10] His awareness of the viability of black power was a powerful incentive to revolution. In a collapsing or oppressive culture such as ours, the incentive to violent revolution is strong among some groups like the Posse Comitatus. For most of us, however, metanoia is more an act of evolutionary rather than revolutionary suicide.

Evolutionary suicide is what we're going to work on now.

First things first: you are going to die whether it's by suicide, homicide, starvation, plague, cancer, or heart failure.

The way things are going, it is highly possible that you will die in the catastrophe that is the death of civilization well before you reach a good old age. Another real possibility is that you will die of a dread disease like Ebola spreading across the earth. Another grim alternative is that you will die as a result of a global collapse of industrialized agriculture and a severe drop in food supply.[11] The way to prepare for your inevitable death or death by evolutionary suicide is to face and own your fear of death psychologically and spiritually.

The place to start is with fears that you are facing right now in the daily rounds of your life. We will look at one way to do that.

When I was earning my living as an organizational development consultant, some clients sought my counsel for personal problems. They came to see me because they were troubled by family or relationship problems, work-related issues, and worries about careers. I began our conversations by asking them to tell me the whole story of their issue or problem. I would then try to paraphrase their issue by saying something like, "So you are worried that your performance review was so bad that your job is in jeopardy?" (Note that this is a statement with a final inflection that tests its accuracy.) Then I would encourage the client to sit quietly and go inside to deepen the pain involved in the issue.

Then I listened to the pain before asking,

"So—if you do get fired, what is the worst thing that can happen?"

"I won't be able to get another job." (I suggest that they deepen the feeling of loss.)

"And, if you can't get another job, what's the worst thing that can happen?" (I suggest that they deepen the feeling of loss.)

"My wife would have to go back to work and I'll become a house husband." (Again deepen the feeling of loss.)

85

"And, if that happened, what would be the worst thing that could happen?"

"What's the worst thing about being a house husband?"

It never failed. We would eventually come to the underlying real fear when the answer was, "The worst thing is that I would die."

Many times the process would end with something like "Actually being a house husband wouldn't be so bad. I might be able to write the novel I have been thinking about." If the conversation reached such a happy prospect so soon, the client would be off and running, perhaps to quit his job or, at least, talk to his wife about quitting and we would not get to the inevitable "The worst thing is that I would die."

When we did get to that end, I said, "That's already settled. You are going to die. Sooner or later you are going to die. Let's get into the deepest fear about your dying." Then we would begin a long discussion exploring the issue with the five stages of death and dying as an outline.

You can try the exercise by yourself in the quiet of your most comfortable room. Doing so might help you see that your fear of death is what generates the other fears and the anxiety that provides the urgency about your more mundane fears.

Take out two or three sheets of paper. No word processor for this task. Handwriting will tend to slow the process and give more time for contemplation. Note: You may have to take the time to work through the stages of grief as you go deeper into your feelings.

---

1. Make a list of all the things that worry you right now, from the silliest to the most global.

2. Then order them in rank from the most to least frightening.

---

3. On another sheet of paper write down your #1 most frightening fear. Think about the losses associated with it and use your imagination to get into the darkest and most painful aspects of the loss. Write them down.

4. Now you can go to the next deeper level of your fears by asking "What would be the worst thing that could happen if that happened?" Then begin a series of steps through the next and next and so on. Give yourself ample time to consider the next worst thing that would happen and allow your deepest feelings to emerge. Note: You may have to take the time to work through the stages of grief as you go deeper into your feelings.

The fear of death is most often a fear of the omnipresent other, the threat of the alien, the terrorist, the natural disaster, the unknown, the abyss, all of the shadowy specters (aka memes) we have erected in our culture and in our inner life.

The fear of death is the handmaiden of the domination system. The Imperium asserts its unique claim to immortality and, using its violent power, instills mortal fears in the minds and hearts of the common people. The Imperium extends a spurious offer of a share of its immortality to the people in exchange for their submission and loyalty.[12]

Honestly facing death; staring it in the face, and letting your fear of it sink deep into you is a gut-wrenching experience. It is, however, the only way to become free of the anxiety jail that most of us live in, and to live an abundant life. Dying to oneself is the first step in metanoia.

An awakening, being born again to an abundant life, just happens. The testimony of those who have had a near-death experience is that they have a wholly new appreciation for a high quality life that had been obscured in their fearful life before death. In a rich post on AlterNet,[13] Fred Branfman lists 13 gifts of death awareness:

Increased aliveness and vitality

A wider range of feeling

Deeper relationships

Increased life-purpose and passion

Wider perspective

Great lucidity and sanity

Greater creativity

Greater compassion and empathy

The courage to be vulnerable

Gratitude, appreciation and awe

Greater aesthetic appreciation

Spiritual openings and the experience of oneness with life

Greater concern for preserving civilization for future generations

If you read Branfman's list carefully, you will see that it is an explication of love. Real love is not the squishy Hollywood version based on mutual narcissism. Love is much deeper and embraces the whole of life's experiences, including the ominous other. Holistic love has one powerful component that isn't obvious and seldom articulated: courage. The opposite of fear is not courage, it is love.

Bill Whittle makes the point this way in this post on his *ejectejecteject* blog in February 2003:[14]

> I've thought a lot about courage in the last few years. And what I've come to realize is that behind courage is a greater emotion still, and that emotion, not surprisingly, is love.

> Think about it. Think of the infantryman who throws himself onto a hand grenade. Perhaps love of country brought him to that time and place. Certainly he loved his family, his wife and children. And more than that, even, he loved his own life, his chance to watch his sons grow into honorable manhood, to give his daughter away in a small church on a Sunday morning.

All of this love may have given him the courage to come to the place where he would face that grenade, but it was his love of his buddies that overcame all of that in that one instant where the heart rules the mind and courage rises unbidden from its mysterious, deep harbor.

Next we are going to explore some of the foundational themes of a new humanity.

---

[1] Elizabeth Kolbert, *The Sixth Extinction: An Unnatural History*, Henry Holt and Co., first edition (February 11, 2014).

[2] For example, see Max Tegmark's book, *Our Mathematical Universe: My Quest for the Ultimate Nature of Reality,* Knopf, 2014.

"Tegmark offers a fascinating exploration of multiverse theories, each one offering new ways to explain 'quantum weirdness' and other mysteries that have plagued physicists, culminating in the idea that our physical world is 'a giant mathematical object' shaped by geometry and symmetry. Tegmark's writing is lucid, enthusiastic, and outright entertaining, a thoroughly accessible discussion leavened with anecdotes and the pure joy of a scientist at work." —*Publishers Weekly*

[3] You may subscribe to Harry T. Cook's Essays at www.harrytcook.com.

[4] Susan Chevalier was an editor at the *Detroit Free Press* for 15 years and is now the managing editor of *JSD,* the bi-monthly journal of Learning Forward, a Dallas-based educational consortium.

[5] Edge #408: The Edge Annual Question 2014: "What Scientific Idea Is Ready For Retirement?" http://www.edge.org/

[6] The moons of Jupiter were discovered by Galileo Galilei around January 1610.

[7] www.seminaryofthestreet.org/ Seminary of the Street is a school for the training of love warriors working toward the transformation of their communities by embodying God's love in the world.

[8] The goals of the Seminary of the Street are ". . . collective liberation from systems of domination, violence, and oppression and the cultivation of alternative communities rooted in tenderness, compassion, love, kindness, generosity, recognition of the sacredness of all life, and awe and wonder at the grandeur of the universe. We recognize that neither liberation nor the creation of alternative community is possible without concurrent transformation within ourselves as we allow the values of the dominant culture to be rooted out of us. In other words, we believe that liberation comes as we struggle toward full aliveness ourselves and align ourselves and our work in the service of life; this then catalyzes aliveness in our communities."

[9] The term derives from the ancient Greek words μετά (metá) (meaning "beyond" or "after") and νόος (noeō) (meaning "perception," "understanding," or "mind").

[10] Huey P. Newton, *Revolutionary Suicide,* Penguin Classics, reprint edition (September 29, 2009).

[11] As I write this a severe drought in California presages a traumatic national shortage of foodstuffs normally produced in the state.

[12] You are a citizen of the immortal fiction called the USA and though you die, yet you live because Amerika lives. It's "Deutschland über alles" all over again. Think also about the promise of Resurrection!

[13] "Embracing Life-Affirming Death Awareness: How to Transform Yourself and Possibly Save Human Civilization," http://alternet.org/, January 22, 2014.

[14] http://www.ejectejecteject.com, February 15, 2003. Bill Whittle is a brilliant and multitalented conservative blogger, a political commentator, director, screenwriter, editor, pilot, and author.

Chapter 9

Creativity begins in your belly or, as we once called it, your soul

Emotion is the messenger of love; it is the vehicle that carries every signal from one brimming heart to another. For human beings, feeling deeply is synonymous with being alive.[1]

WE, THAT IS TO SAY the human race, have tried what we called civilization for about 10,000 years and it is now in its death throes. Civilization as a form of human organization conforms to a fundamental process of the universe. Things are born or created, grow, live, strive, diminish, and die. Civilization is dying of its disease, the domination system.

Now it is time to try something new. Since human beings created civilization, we can now give birth to a new form of social organization. The first steps in the birthing process begin with you, a unique individual with the power to change the way you think, the way you attend to your basic emotional needs, and the way you relate to others.

Evolutionary suicide is not a one-time event; it is a process that takes place over time as you become more and more aware of the bits and pieces of your mind that you need to shrive. Evolutionary suicide presents the promise of a life free from your captivity in the memes[2] that lock us into the culture of civilization. By committing evolutionary suicide you can free yourself from the culturally dominant demands of an endless search for security, status, wealth, and power. Those four words are the headings for a host of memes that are fundamental to the perpetuation of the domination/violence core of civilization. The process of evolutionary suicide is to allow those memes to die and new memes to be born.

So let's assume that you're working at committing evolutionary suicide. You are burying old memes like "be strong, assertive, aggressive, be a winner, don't quit, be tough" and you are ready to attach to some new memes that support the creation of a new you and a new humanity. We are going to start where you do have power: in your soul, your belly.

First we consider love—love one another, love life, love makes the world go round.

Jungian therapist and author Jean Shinoda Bolen has said,

> It's been my impression that we all come into the world as children who want love, and if we can't get love, we settle for power. On a personal level, once power becomes the ruling archetype in the man's (or woman's) psyche, that person's choices are made to achieve position, keep power, look good and be in control.[3]

Bolen's impression is a neat Jungian précis of the work of Thomas Lewis, Fari Amini, and Richard Lannon as they described it in *A General Theory of Love*. They say that children come into the world not only wanting love, but having an absolute need for it.

This review by Carol Mann in *Publishers Weekly* (which appears on Amazon's page on the book) captures the essence of the authors' thesis.

The Beatles may have sounded naïve when they assured us that "all you need is love," but they may not have been far off the mark. New research in brain function has proven that love is a human necessity; its absence damages not only individuals, but our whole society. In this stimulating work, psychiatrists Lewis, Amini and Lannon explain how and why our brains have evolved to require consistent bonding and nurturing.

They contend that close emotional connections actually change neural patterns in those who engage in them, affecting our sense of self and making empathy and socialization possible. Indeed, the authors insist, "in some important ways, people cannot be stable on their own."

Yet American society is structured to frustrate emotional health, they contend: self-sufficiency and materialistic goals are seen as great virtues, while emotional dependence is considered a weakness. Because our culture does not sufficiently value interpersonal relationships, we are plagued by anxiety and depression, narcissism and superficiality, which can lead to violence and self-destructive behaviors.

It is futile to try to think our way out of such behaviors, the authors believe, because emotions are not within the intellect's domain. What is needed is healthy bonding from infancy; when this does not occur, the therapist must model it. The authors' utopian vision of emotional health may strike some as vague or conservative to a fault, and the clarity of their thesis is marred by indirect and precious writing. Yet their claim that "what we do inside relationships matters more than any other aspect of human life" is a powerful one.

And as Thomas Lewis tells us,

The capacious and monocular neocortical brain tells us that ideas perpetuate civilization. The thick marble walls of libraries and museums protect our supposed bequest to future ages. How short a vision. Our children are the builders of tomorrow's world—quiet infants, clumsy toddlers, and running, squealing second-graders, whose pliable neurons carry within them all humanity's hope. Their flexible brains have yet to germinate the ideas, the songs, the societies of tomorrow.

93

They can create the next world or they can annihilate it. In either case, they will do so in our names.[4]

To love is to emit positive life-affirming emotional energy that moves outward from the belly, the seat of the soul, toward another being or beings. Sometimes the feeling of love happens in a brief shared positive moment. The feeling of love can be spontaneous and happens to us in surprising ways. It can be generated out of an intuitive sense, a burst of biological lust, or a response to being unexpectedly loved. In other times it may be generated by an act of will as when you say, "This person really needs my loving support." When love is reciprocated, its positive effect on both or all parties is exponential. When love is unrequited, the effect can be devastating. One of the reasons that we love dogs and other animals is that they have no problem returning love. Animals love because they operate out of their limbic brains and the limbic brain does not make "rational judgments."

The secondary gain in loving relationships is trust. I trust my wife, my kids because I love them and they love me and in that love we take care of one another. When love prevails in any system, trust grows and the ability of that system to develop healthy outcomes expands exponentially.

Many years ago I had the privilege of learning about the exponential power of love and trust from Jack Gibb, the creator of TORI theory. He used the acronym TORI for Trust, Openness, Realization, and Interdependence. I met Jack at a weekend workshop where he was presenting his theory and method in an interactive group format. One of the first exercises he introduced was a very simple way of experiencing love. We each chose a partner and then sat on the floor opposite one another, cross-legged, with our knees touching. We were instructed to be silent and look into each other's eyes for five minutes.

The experience was powerful. Almost every one of the 75 or so people in the room experienced a profound caring connection with their partner. In the next exercise we worked in groups of six. Each group was to come to a decision about what we would like to have happen for the rest of the weekend. The group members experienced a startling level of trust in one another. It was as though the loving relationship that occurred in pairs and in the sextets set the climate for trust in the whole assembly. The rest of the weekend was an experiential demonstration of the power of TORI to reach profound group consensus without any manifestations of hierarchical leadership.

When love and trust are foundational in a group of almost any size, and when people are self-disclosing, open, and honest with one another, they become more responsible for the well-being of the whole group and everyone becomes dependent on everyone else.

At one time, Jack was called on to work with the entire staff and faculty of a university to help them discern the way to deal with a crisis in their system. He gathered the group in the university football stadium and led the crowd through a variation of the exercises I had experienced during that weekend. At the end of a long day they reached community consensus on what needed to happen next to move beyond the crisis. Moreover, almost every one of them felt they owned a piece of the outcome and were committed to achieving it.[5]

The primary characteristics of civilization are domination and violence. The primary characteristics of a new humanity are love and equality. When your discipline of evolutionary suicide enables you to die to the memes of survival through domination and security through violence, you are on the way to freedom and creativity.

One of the memes embedded in us through the practice of civilization tells us that it is important to use power to succeed in reaching your goals of security, status, and wealth. Power memes in our culture are most visible when we look at the way in which boys are socialized. The ideal of manliness is not to feel any hurt, or if you feel hurt to conceal it. When a boy is hurt he hears, "Pick yourself up, dust yourself off, and get back in the game." The object of whatever game is on the field is to win by beating the other guys. The power memes are revealed when regressive cadres (male and sadly, female) in our civilized culture are fixated on male domination of women. The movement to eliminate abortion and access to contraception is probably one of the most disgusting manifestations of the male need to dominate women.

The old dominance memes disparage love and mutual care in favor of hostility toward the other with whom we are (necessarily, by nature?) in conflict. Now the way to protect yourself even in church in the state of Georgia is with a gun. Our old memes associate power with domination and violence; loving and empathetic behavior is labeled as weak and counterproductive. We need to reframe power to understand it in relation to love and mutual care.

Working and writing in the same era as Jack Gibb, Rollo May, an American existentialist psychologist, explored the nature of power. In a book called *Power and Innocence*[6] he presented what he had learned about power. His definition of power was very simple: It is the ability to cause or prevent change.[7]

He identified five escalating levels of power.[8]

1) The power to be—the driving force for life that inheres in all beings; the drive for existence.

2) The power of self-affirmation—is the force that drives us to be valued and esteemed as significant for who we are.

3) The power of self-assertion—is invoked against threats to my being and affirmation as well as threats to my own people from our enemies.

4) The power of aggression is—invoked when my self-assertion is not effective.

5) The power of violence—is used when all avenues to affirmation are blocked and aggressive reasoning and persuasion ineffectual.

As I think about this escalating scale, it seems to me that May was caught in the culture of civilization because his thesis seems to assume that a person must achieve powerful, self-worthy autonomy as a defense against being dismissed or overcome by others. If he had become familiar with Jack Gibb's work, he might have seen that when people work openly and honestly at levels 1, 2, and 3, they realize the commonality in their lives, and they are aware of the wholeness and richness in themselves and in one another.

May also identifies five kinds of power potentially present in every person:[9]

1) Exploitative: subjects the weak to the strong with no concern for the needs of the weak, and tends to identify power with violence.

2) Manipulative: power over another that requires the collusion, collaboration, and cooperation of the weaker, probably out of some need in the weaker party of which the stronger may be aware.

3) Competitive: power against another when the object is to win, but the win/lose set tends to shrink the community

within which it takes place. This is the only kind of power that mixes the destructive and creative forces. For example, a music competition may stimulate composers to write excellent music and may make for vitality even though there may be many losers.

4) Nutrient: power used for the other to meet the needs of the other.

5) Synergistic: power used with another to build a better life for both. Produces an effect greater than the sum of all separate effects: Makes power available to the community and uses the power of all.

I suggest there is a sixth kind of power. Subversive power undermines the other by indirect, non-confrontational, and nonviolent means that may include such things as ridicule, public humiliation, peaceful demonstrations, sit-down strikes, and a host of other behaviors and actions. In his book *From Dictatorship to Democracy: A Conceptual Framework for Liberation*,[10] Gene Sharp identified "198 Methods of Non-Violent Action," most of which are subversive.

Love is a power that is inherent in us and accessible to be the foundation on which the new post-civilized culture may be built.

Someone wisely said that the only thing that you can change is yourself. You do have the power to cause some and prevent other changes in the world, but you are limited on your own. You need the help of others to cause or prevent change in the world.

We need to look at how a personal commitment to the power of love and trust can be manifested and linked with others to make significant changes in the way the world works. That's next.

[1] Thomas Lewis, Fari Anini, and Richard Lannon, *A General Theory of Love* (Vintage), Knopf Doubleday Publishing Group, Kindle Edition, 2007, p. 35.

[2] *meme:* an element of a culture or system of behavior that may be considered to be passed from one individual or group to another by nongenetic means, esp. imitation.

[3] Jean Shinoda Bolen, *Gods in Everyman,* Harpercollins Publisher, 1989.

[4] Op. cit., p. 223.

[5] Jack Gibb's book, *Trust: A New View of Personal and Organizational Development* (1978) is out of print. It is available online at http://www.oocities.org/toritrust/index.html.

[6] Rollo May, *Power and Innocence,* W. W. Norton & Co. Inc., 1972. His other works include *Love and Will, The Meaning of Anxiety,* and *The Courage to Create.*

[7] May op. cit., p. 99.

[8] May op. cit., p. 40 ff.

[9] May op. cit., p. 105 ff.

[10] Gene Sharp, "From Dictatorship to Democracy: A Conceptual Framework for Liberation," 4th ed., 2010, pamphlet.

Chapter 10

Some inner dynamics of love, trust, and openness

If your view of the world is that people use reason for their important decisions, you are setting yourself up for a life of frustration and confusion.

You'll find yourself continually debating people and never winning except in your own mind.

Few things are as destructive and limiting as a worldview that assumes people are mostly rational.

—Scott Adams, creator of Dilbert

THEORETICALLY, OR BETTER, hopefully, you have committed evolutionary suicide. You know that you are dying as you live and that death to the old memes that were generated and are sustained by the domination system means you are free to live in a new and wonderful way.

The primary meme in your new life is love, the force that binds us to one another and to all the phenomenal others. Being immersed in love means that you love and cherish your whole being, those immediately around you, and those with whom you share life's experiences even though they may be on the opposite side of the globe. When you love and you cherish, you make yourself vulnerable. Then you are prepared to trust the processes of the universe that gave you birth, sustained you, and brought you to the place where you can read these lines. You can trust that though you die, yet you may live.

When Jack Gibb writes about openness, he is suggesting that we trust enough to let every bit of our experience be available to one another. Trust and openness means that we can expose to others the places where we are most vulnerable and we can accept others when they expose their most vulnerable places.[1]

During my three careers, I worked with many groups, both newly forming groups and intact groups in many organizational settings: schools, corporations (manufacture, utilities and retailing), nonprofits, and churches. Whether it was a newly forming or intact group, every group I worked with was a new group, not only for me, but also for everyone there. Although most people in a group may have known and worked with one another for some time, I was a new member of their group. It was, therefore, a new group.

I discovered a really efficient way to develop trust and openness in a new group. I started by asking them to look around the room in which we were meeting to see if they thought it was a safe place to be. Then I asked them to look at every other person in the room in turn and ask themselves if it was safe to be with that person. Next I asked if any one felt unsafe with these people, and if there was someone who felt unsafe we stopped to deal with that issue.

The next step was to ask them to do a few minutes of silent inner work to identify the worst thing they had ever done in life. After a few minutes I asked them to dig even deeper to see if there wasn't something even worse than that. When they seemed certain that they had reached the very worst thing they had ever done, I suggested that they identify the second worst and the third worst and maybe even the fourth worst thing they had ever done.

After the period of silence I told them that we were going to go around the room, sun-wise (that's clockwise) and each person would share the second or third worst thing they ever did *but they were not to disclose the worst thing.* I always went first. That was easy because I have a Sears catalog collection of second-worst things I ever did. I also said that the general rule in all our work together was that they had the freedom to simply pass on their turn and not respond.

It never failed. I don't know for certain if people actually did it consistently, but when I asked people privately in breaks at the end of the exercise if they had shared the worst or the second worst or third worst, they told me they'd shared the worst.

By the time we had gone around the entire group, the level of interpersonal trust in the group was astonishing. After the third or fourth person spoke we were able to identify in ourselves similar situations and our feelings about it tended to be identical and empathic. We quickly reached that point in TORI theory called Realization. We realized that we are all valuable and we are all vulnerable and we all have the power to go on. In that realization we are stronger together. Trust and openness bring about an environment that Jack Gibb called High Quality. HQ environments bring about high quality human life.[2] I will have more to say in another chapter about the evolutionary power of high quality group process.

I hope you have seen the connection between the self-disclosure involved in telling people about the second-worst thing you've ever done in your life and the emotional content and impact of that disclosure. Feelings around self-disclosure are things like embarrassment, humility, shame, inadequacy, guilt, and stupidity. Those feelings arise out of our desire to be well thought of and embraced by those around us. We want our chosen people to think that we are fulfilling our ideals and operating according to the values of the group. This is true for a young gang member who feels challenged to gain his peers' acceptance by beating up someone weaker than himself. It's true for the CEO who has a constant need to parade her self-identified competence before those who look up to her. It's also true for the aspiring politician whose real position on an issue is disclosed by an unauthorized video recording that exhibits his venality and hypocrisy.

Honest self-disclosure by the gang member, the CEO, and the politician might reveal some very different emotions than those displayed in the public marketplace. Each of them is probably scared to death of rejection, uncertain about his or her persona and psyche, and feeling incompetent.

It's ironic that the energy we use to adopt social roles that will display our certainty, our confidence, and our competence is generated by some of the fundamental memes in the culture of our violence/domination civilization. How much easier it might be to honestly disclose to one another the fact that we have these negative emotions and put the energy we save into working together. Working together in trust and openness from the same foundation is liberation from the culture of violence and power.[3]

In a trusting climate, openness is the ability to tell stories about my experience with all the facts, figures, and emotions embedded in them. When you tell me a story about how you learned that you had a cancerous malignancy and then tell me all about the stages of treatment and care that have enabled you to survive until now, the facts and figures may be hard to comprehend. What touches me, moves me, energizes me, and connects me with you are the feelings that the story arouses in me.

Most folks don't realize that they have three brains in their skulls, one on top of the other, all connected and all working to make human life unique.[4]

The brain stem is the primitive reptilian brain (archipallium); it's the same as the whole brain of an alligator or a snake. It's the brain that keeps your heart beating, your lungs pumping, your gastrointestinal system working, and causes you to jump into the air in fright when a car comes through your bedroom. It also energizes the body for fight, to lash out physically at the drunk behind the wheel, or to flee (run next door to call 911). Your primitive brain is a good thing to have around. It's important to remember that the snake who lives in you is your ally and friend.

The limbic brain (the paleopallium) that wraps around the brain stem is an evolutionary development in primitive mammals. It is the part of the brain that evokes agreeable and disagreeable reactions. It stimulates females to nurse and children to develop playfulness. It is the seat of our emotions and feelings, like wrath, fright, passion, love, hate, joy, and sadness. Our limbic brains are powerful. A growing body of knowledge and research says that the decisions you make are basically determined by your emotions, your feelings—by your limbic brain. This affective domain is the predominant factor in what connects us with other humans and with beasts.[5]

The third brain (the neopallium) developed with the beginnings of us, the so-called superior mammals. The rational third brain is a complex net of neural cells that enabled symbolic language, the subsequent ability to develop intellectual tasks such as reading, writing, performing mathematical calculations, and engaging in abstract thought. The function of rational thought is to rationalize the emotional choices you make and dream up alternative futures.

Because of the civilization mindset (culture) that is a collection of memes that exalt hierarchy and domination, the neopallium is taken to be the dominant brain of the three in your skull. It is not dominant, however, when the reptilian brain or the limbic brain takes charge. The experience of many salespeople says exactly the opposite. The limbic brain rules. Realtors will tell you that clients often come to them with a list of the "must haves" in a home they are seeking. After seeing many homes that meet their criteria, the "must have" list will go right out the window when they walk into a house with few, if any, of the features on their list and immediately say, "This is our house. It feels so right." Neopallium be damned. The limbic brain wins every time.

We need to note two things. The first is that the limbic brain needs nurturing to help with its development. Children who receive lots of loving and affection in positive relationships in the early years of life turn out to be more mentally healthy than children who do not.[6]

The second is that when the gifts and contributions of the three brains are not honored and recognized for their full capacity or are dismissed and denied, they can rise up out of your shadow side and hurt you and your relationships. Here's what Dr. Stephen Diamond, a forensic psychologist, says about the shadow side.[7]

> Whatever we deem evil, inferior or unacceptable and deny in ourselves becomes part of the shadow, the counterpoint to what Jung called the persona or conscious ego personality. According to Jungian analyst Aniela Jaffe, the shadow is the "sum of all personal and collective psychic elements which, because of their incompatibility with the chosen conscious attitude, are denied expression in life."[8]

There are ways to acknowledge, own, and integrate your shadow into your self-concept, so that your shadow will not rise up and sabotage you at the least-expected moments. One way to get to know your shadow is to think about two or three people you really despise, or can't stand. Think about their behaviors and characteristics that make your skin crawl. Those are the behaviors and characteristics of your shadow. Then you need to look at how they might bring strengths to your life. Your reptilian brain can and will save you from all kinds of accidents. Your limbic brain can lead you into a world of delights. Own and embrace and integrate your shadow. You will begin to see how it will help you to a more rich and abundant experience of life.

When you deny the gift of your snake brain to react immediately to a threat by fighting or fleeing, and the snake senses a threat even from your beloved, it will come out of the shadow, out of the hidden place, out of the dark, and devour your beloved.

When you deny the gift of your limbic brain that seeks to build warm relationships and you are fighting with a person, your mammalian brain may come out of the shadow and reveal your Achilles heel, the warmth and gentleness of your innocent child.

When you deny the gift of your rational brain and are cruising along in sure and certain confidence of your ability to understand a situation better than anyone around, your shadow side may leap out and do or say something utterly stupid to sabotage your conscious ego.

In a trusting climate, openness is the ability not only to disclose your emotions, but also your dreams, fantasies, and nightmares, those thoughts, images, and word plays that evoke a different dimension to the reality in which we find ourselves. Are you fantasizing about the catastrophe that will come to your low-lying San Francisco neighborhood in a few hundred years? Are you fantasizing about moving from San Francisco to the Sierra Nevada in a few years? Are you feeling defeated by images of trying to raise your own food? Are you dreaming about a long-term relationship with a beautiful beloved?

In a loving, trusting climate, openness is the ability to let it all hang out and to realize the intimate connection of all things. It permits us to create and develop a new kind of human community liberated from of the constraints (the values, rules, memes) of the violence/domination civilization.

Next we are going to work on the personal foundation for creating a new kind of human community.

---

[1] TORI Theory holds that when there is a high level of Trust we are freed up to be ourselves, dropping roles and positions. This naturally leads to Openness—information flows between people; people say what they think, know, need, and care about. Trust and openness lead to Realization—people express and create in ways that are deeply meaningful. When groups have high levels of trust, openness, and realization, they naturally mature into higher levels of Interdependence, boundaries blur, and there is ever more synergy and effectiveness.

[2] As you will see in a later chapter, I call HQ groups "HA," High Affect Groups.

[3] The opposite of violence is not obsequiousness or submissiveness. The opposite is peaceability, which includes tenderness, kindness, and amiability, virtues that require great power and discipline.

[4] Recent neuroscientific research with lower mammals seems to indicate that the human brain is not quite as unique as it was once thought to be.

[5] The best horse whisperers like Tom Dorrance and Ray Hunt have a difficult time putting what they do into words because they relate to horses limbic brain-to limbic brain. Since it is not rational, their rational descriptions do not describe what really happens in their whispering. Like many practitioners, how they do their craft is different from their rational descriptions of it.

[6] See Thomas Lewis, Fari Amini, and Richard Lannon, *A General Theory of Love* (Vintage), Knopf Doubleday Publishing Group, 2007, Kindle Edition.

[7] Stephen Diamond, *Anger, Madness, and the Daimonic: The Psychological Genesis of Violence, Evil, and Creativity,* SUNY Press, 1996.

[8] Diamond was particularly interested in evil. Other psychologists recognize that the good can also be hidden in the shadow.

Chapter 11

Foundational love

Love is omni-inclusive, progressively exquisite, understanding and compassionately attuned to other than self.

—*Richard Buckminster Fuller*

IN ORDER TO BUILD a new human community we have to begin with the reality of the self. Our fate as human beings is to be pilloried on the antitheses of our biological drive for survival and our amazing ability to fantasize, to imagine ourselves as immortal. We struggle between the drives of the brain stem and the neocortex. This struggle will be our fate until there is a profoundly radical change in our genetic makeup. Since that may only happen centuries from now, we are left with the option of changing the memes that shape culture.

Fear is at the core of the power that the old memes have over us. If we are locked in fear about our survival, each of us will seek power over others and over our natural and cultural environment. We will attempt to secure our survival by defending our status in the hierarchy and accumulating a wealth of personal and material assets. Living in fear means that we affirm and submit to the principal memes of the domination system: individualism,[1] fear, security, status, wealth, and power.[2]

Fear keeps you locked in your place in the hierarchy of the domination system, whether you are the dictator or you are the lowest of the low. Having died, however, there is nothing more to fear. You have given up your life and there is nothing more to evoke fear in you. That means that the most you suffer will come from your willingness to empathize with any who suffer.

Now as we face the collapse of civilization and perhaps the end of human life, it is necessary to find the best ways to adapt to change through the end times. And in surviving the collapse, we will need to create communities and a new humanity.

I am assuming that you have seriously begun the process of evolutionary suicide and are working at it on a daily basis. I hope that you are dying to the principal memes of the domination/violence system and are embracing some of the alternative memes that undergird a post-civilization humanity.

You may remember Ben Whittle's discovery that behind courage, the opposite of fear, is love. You may also remember that the basis of trust is love.[3] What help is there for those of us who want to become less fearful and more trusting, who want to become more loving and caring people?

The first thing to do is to go down to your favorite bookstore or get on the Internet, buy two books and read them.

1) I introduced you to *A General Theory of Love*[4] in Chapter 6.

2) Now I introduce you to *Love 2.0: How Our Supreme Emotion Affects Everything We Feel, Think, Do, and Become* by Barbara Fredrickson, who has been studying positive emotions for decades. She explores what love is on a physical,

bodily, neurobiological level. In *Love 2.0* she tells how her research expands our knowledge and experience of love.

Here's a taste of her wisdom.

Longing. You know the feeling. It's that ache of sensing that something vital is missing from your life; a deep thirst for more. More meaning, more connection, more energy—more something. Longing is that feeling that courses through your body just before you decide that you're restless, lonely, or unhappy.[5]

What you long for is love. Whether you're single or not, whether you spend your days largely in isolation or steadily surrounded by the buzz of conversation, love is the essential nutrient that your cells crave: true positivity-charged connection with other living beings.[6]

The vision of love that I offer here will require a radical shift, a departure from what you've come to believe. It's time to upgrade your view of love.[7]

First and foremost, love is an emotion, a momentary state that arises to infuse your mind and body alike. Love, like all emotions, surfaces like a distinct and fast-moving weather pattern, a subtle and ever-shifting force. As for all positive emotions, the inner feeling love brings you is inherently and exquisitely pleasant. The boundaries between you and not-you—what lies beyond your skin—relax and become more permeable. While infused with love you see fewer distinctions between you and others. Indeed, your ability to see others—really see them, wholeheartedly—springs open. Love can even give you a palpable sense of oneness and connection, a transcendence that makes you feel part of something far larger than yourself.[8]

To put it in a nutshell, love is the momentary upwelling of three tightly interwoven events: first, a sharing of one or more positive emotions between you and another; second, a synchrony between your and the other person's biochemistry and behaviors; and third, a reflected motive to invest in each other's well-being that brings mutual care. My shorthand for this trio is positivity resonance. Within those moments of interpersonal connection that are characterized by this amplifying symphony—of shared positive emotions, biobehavioral synchrony, and mutual care—life-giving positivity resonates between and among people. This back-and-forth reverberation of positive energy sustains itself—and can even grow stronger—until the momentary connection wanes, which is of course inevitable, because that's how emotions work.[9]

The single most important reason to buy Fredrickson's book is to access the *Lovingkindness Meditations* that cannot be reproduced here. The meditations stimulate growth in our ability to love. Her strategies are based in significant research and represent the most profound effort to embed new love memes that are the foundation for building the kind of relationships necessary for the end times. You may also find guided meditations on her website.[10] Here is the Index of Practices from page 206 of her book.

Micro-moment Practices[11]
Reflect on Your Social Connections
Create Three Loving Connections
Narrate Your Day with Acceptance and Kindness
Use Your Own Suffering as a Cue to Connect
Create Compassion in Daily Life
Create Celebratory Love in Daily Life
Reconstruct Your Yesterday to Uncover Opportunities for
    Love
Redesign Your Job Around Love
Meditation Practices
Loving-Kindness
See Yourself as the Target of Others' Love
Self-Love
Compassionate Love
Celebratory Love
Loving All

Let's suppose that you experience a life-sustaining reverberation between you and a person you have just met. You both found pleasure in that momentary relationship. You connected. You would like to repeat it. You'd like to make it into something you might experience time and again. How can you make that happen? How can you turn that once-experienced relationship into a friendship? How can you become a neighbor to that new acquaintance?

I take my clues from Jess Lair, who wrote a book called *"I ain't well—but I sure am better": Mutual Need Therapy*[12] and from one of the top 20 most popular TED talks, Brené Brown's 2010 talk[13] on the power of vulnerability.

Make a list of all the people in your life with whom you had that kind of momentary loving experience. You may have to work at making the list over a course of days or weeks. When that list is done, check-mark the people on the list who are always glad to see you no matter how bad they feel. From among those you checked, check-mark all those who you are always glad to see no matter how bad you feel. From that double-checked list pick five people. Those five are most likely your very best friends.

If possible, make face-to-face contact with one or more of those five people every week. Sit down for lunch or coffee or take a walk with them and let it all hang out. By that I mean tell them about your inner life, your emotions as you have experienced a low and a high in the past week or 10 days. Tell a brief story including explicit words about your feelings. You are *not* seeking sympathy. Then shut up, smile at them, listen to them, and attempt to feel their emotions. In feeling one another's emotions, oneness is experienced and true connections are made.[14]

What you are doing with this process is building the kind of relationships, the friendships that make up a true neighborhood, an intimate sharing community. It's a neighborhood that doesn't necessarily involve living on the same street or the same part of the city or working for the same company. It transcends limitation.

In order to create a new humanity through the end times, we have to start with loving relationships and then we have to build loving communities. The key to sustaining loving communities is that the inner life, which consists of feelings about everything—dreams, hopes, pleasures, anxieties, and fears—is shared openly and easily in a climate of acceptance and affirmation. That describes the openness that Jack Gibb discovered in his work. Openness leads to trust. Trust leads to responsibility. Responsibility leads to interdependence and interdependence leads to people working together on their mutual concerns and interests.

When a positive love experience happens between two of you, or in a small group, there is another profound outcome. You experience parity, the state of being equal.

Those who are captive to the memes of civilization may talk about all people being equal, but the reality of their relationships reveals a mutual evaluation about each person's place in the social hierarchy. When two people meet for the first time their tendency is to ask questions like "What do you do?" (Meaning what work do you do or where you do it?) "Where do you live?" Even before the questions begin, there is a subtle evaluation of place in the social structure based on style, clothing, demeanor, and accent. Have you noticed how often Australian or English accents are used in voiceovers in television advertising? Or how in ads for big trucks, the voiceover is often a deep-voiced Texas or Oklahoma accent?

Parity is the name that I give to compassionate relationships in which we have a deep mutual awareness of our common situation in life. Parity is recognizing that all of us have the same stake in life, that we are all in this together and it is both precarious and profoundly beautiful.

Parity has an even deeper dimension. It is the recognition that the other really counts, really matters, deserves and should get my commitment to serve and to help him or her to a richer and more beautiful life.

Since we have committed evolutionary suicide and are working to perfect it, we can now abandon any notion of surviving as selves and focus on the well-being of others.

---

[1] Our heritage from the Enlightenment and the age of science and industry has given us a new twist on the domination syndrome of civilization. We now exalt individualism to the place where whole cadres of oligarchs and their retainers believe that greed is good and that following Ayn Rand's philosophy (if it can be dignified enough to be called such) is a worthwhile life choice. The only way I can understand the intense commitment to the selfishness inherent in individualism is to see it as a reaction to a subliminal awareness of the threat inherent in the apocalypse of civilization. Greed is at the apotheosis of values in the culture of domination/violence. Greed is also a dysfunctional antidote to the fear of death through deprivation. From the top to the bottom of the hierarchy in the domination system, fear is a prevailing emotion. The cry of the lonely politician says it best: "If I don't go along with the system my political (i.e., whole) life is dead."

[2] Kirk Schneider, "Why Are Humans Violent? The Psychological Reason We Hurt Each Other," Alternet, July 30, 2014:

"As a depth psychologist with many years of experience, I can say emphatically that the sense of being crushed, humiliated and existentially unimportant are the main factors behind so much that we call psychopathology.

"Why would it not follow that the same factors are at play in social and cultural upheavals? The emerging science of 'terror management theory' shows convincingly that when people feel unimportant they equate those feelings with dying—and they will do everything they can, including becoming extreme and destructive themselves to avoid that feeling.

"The sense of insignificance and death anxiety have been shown to play a key role in everything from terrorism to mass shootings to extremist religious and political ideologies to obsessions with materialism and wealth. Just about all that is violent and corrupt in our world seems connected to it."

[3] Both from Chapter 8.

[4] by Fari Amini, Richard Lannon, and Lewis Thomas, MD.

[5] op. cit., p. 3.

[6] op. cit., p.4.

[7] op. cit., p. 5.

[8] op. cit., pp.15–16.

[9] op. cit., p. 17.

[10] http://www.positivityresonance.com/meditations.html

[11] op. cit., p. 206.

[12] Jess Lair, *"I ain't well — but I sure am better": Mutual Need Therapy*, Doubleday, 1975.

[13] http://www.ted.com/talks/brene_brown_on_vulnerability?utm_source=newsletter_weekly_2011-01-04&utm_campaign=newsletter_weekly&utm_medium=email

[14] "Interestingly, the simple act of sharing an important secret from your life with someone you just met increases your naturally circulating levels of oxytocin, which in turn raises your confidence that you can trust that person to guard your privacy. Thankfully, we also know that oxytocin does not induce trust indiscriminately, making people gullible and therefore open to exploitation. The effects of oxytocin on trust turn out to be quite sensitive to interpersonal cues, like those subtle signs that tip you off that another may be the gambling type or irresponsible in other ways. Rest assured, then, if oxytocin spray were to be aerated through your workplace ventilation system, you'd still maintain your shrewd attunement to subtle signs that suggest whether someone is worthy of your trust or not." —Barbara Fredrickson, *Love 2.0: Finding Happiness and Health in Moments of Connection,* Penguin Group US, Kindle Edition 2013, p. 50.

Chapter 12

The natural world

In nature's economy the currency is not money. It is life.

Seeds and eggs are the most valuable things in the currency of life.

—Beehive Collective[1]

BARBARA FREDRICKSON has done amazing work in understanding the neuropsychology of love, and a key to her work lies in the term *positivity resonance.* That term describes the experience of a loving connection. In order to expand awareness of the potential of positivity resonance, Fredrickson created meditations specifically to help us extend our love toward wider human networks. Moving beyond her work, we need to enhance our ability to love, to experience positivity resonance with the entire creation, particularly sentient life.

Love begins with the willingness to be open about our deepest feelings and sensitive to hearing the feelings behind our companion's words. So we reiterate two thematic terms, trust and openness. Mutual empathy is another way of describing a love relationship.

Any dog lover or horse whisperer will tell you that it is possible to have a mutual empathetic relationship, a relationship of trust and openness with an animal. Mutuality is probably more difficult with a cat, but it is possible to have a one-way relationship of trust and openness. You can relate to a cat with empathy and compassion without expecting the cat to have any regard for you whatsoever.

If you've been following Facebook or YouTube, you've probably seen examples of inter-species behavior that seems to indicate empathic relationships. One extended video clip revealed the nature of a relationship between a small dog and an elephant who were confined together in a large field at rescue facility. When the dog got sick and was brought indoors, the elephant became agitated and stayed as close as possible to the building where the dog was hospitalized. Although the dog had not fully recovered, the keepers decided to let the dog out. The elephant was shown stroking the dog with its trunk welcoming the dog. The dog quickly recovered. There was also an incident that took place off the California coast when a team set out to release a whale from the fishing net in which it was entangled. After the team succeeded, they expected the whale would immediately race off in search of its pod. Much to their surprise, the whale came up alongside their boat and rubbed against it several times as if to say thank you.

Most people seem to regard such interspecies relationships as exceptional, unique, and certainly not normal. I suggest that's because they are observing the phenomena from a domination system perspective. Viewed from a different perspective, it seems like it might be a normal phenomenon when the animals involved are not under environmental distress.

It is clear to people who are involved in the study of human communication that only 5% or 10% of our interaction is auditory. Most of our communication takes place at a nonverbal level, which involves visual and affective data. The limbic brain, or as Philip Shepherd calls it, the brain in the belly, is at work.

I had the good fortune to participate in a workshop designed by my friend and neighbor, Ariana Strozzi. She has developed a remarkable process in which she uses horses to help professionals in many fields better understand the subtleties of their management styles and helps them shift to more effective methods. Managers and leaders who rely primarily on their limbic brains form close relationships with horses quickly. Those whose principle modes are verbal and auditory have a much harder time connecting with the horses.

It is fascinating to watch the process. Each of us was asked to enter a round pen in which a horse was confined. When one woman walked into the round pen, the horse moved over to the gate as far from her as possible. When she moved toward the horse it avoided her. She tried a number of different approaches, but the horse was not cooperating. When she gave up in frustration and walked way, the horse softened and moved toward her. As Ariana talked with her about what had happened, the woman realized it was a paradigm of her management style.[2]

Positivity resonance with animals, which is to say loving relationships with animals, are manifest when we relate to them with our limbic brains.

I would like to suggest that you experiment with loving relationships to things like bees. A little anthropomorphizing may help. A dose of wonder and mindfulness will also help.

Sometime just watch a bee move from one blossom to another and feel that in your belly. Imagine what it's like to be that bee. As they say in Gestalt therapy, "Be the bee."

Watch young barn swallows learning to fly so they can nourish themselves by catching insects in the air. Imagine what it's like to be that bird. Be the barn swallow. Describe to yourself what it's like as the bird. "I am unsure and I don't change directions well. . . . ah, now I have it . . . wow!"

One further exercise: Next time you see an ant, or a spider or woolly bear crawling across the pavement, do the same exercise. Work on it to see if you can develop a positivity resonance with birds and bees and insects and woolly bears.

Sometimes I read about someone saying with great authority that animals have no intentions and no feelings, and I wonder, "Doesn't this guy have a dog?"

—Frans de Waal

Years ago I read about research that was done to determine if there was a positive effect of love on plants. Loving energy was sent to some plants, not to others in the same greenhouse beds. Would the plants that were loved be healthier than plants that were not? As I recall, the researchers determined that, yes, plants showered with love grew better. The best single source of information is a 2013 *New Yorker* article by Michael Pollan.[3]

I am not a gardener, and unlike devoted gardeners, I find it difficult to remember to love the tomato plants that are growing in my hay bale garden. I do not experience any reciprocal love when I remember to do it. I don't have a mutual affective relationship with my tomato plants until I chew on a mature tomato and get a real positivity sensation.

If the future of humankind in this century is nearly as grim as many climatologists predict, it will be necessary to develop the skills to engage in a collaborative relationship with whatever parts of the natural world survive. When the major structures of civilization have collapsed, and when the era of peak oil is ended, the surviving humans will need to nourish themselves on what they can grow and what they can hunt and gather. The survivors will have to learn to interact with grace and generosity with the plant and animal life found in their environment.

Humans of the late 21st century will have to learn the skills of indigenous peoples and Neolithic hunter/gatherers to finds gentle ways to provision us without resorting to domination/violence methods. We will need to remember the practice of Zen woodworkers who spend hours of their time waiting until they are certain that the tree is willing to be cut down to make the lumber needed for a project. We will need to remember the task of the Pawnee buffalo medicine man whose yearlong meditation is focused on locating the area where the herd will be grazing at the time of the hunt and determining when the herd is ready to give up some of its members so the tribe may live.

The process of learning the new/old ways is already underway by people who are developing sustainable agriculture[4] through such things as edible forest gardens, permaculture, consumer supported agriculture (CSA), and the Locavore movement.[5]

Edible Forest Gardens

An edible forest garden is a perennial polyculture of multipurpose plants—many species growing together (a polyculture), most plants re-growing every year without needing to be re-planted (perennials), each plant contributing to the success of the whole by fulfilling many functions. In other words, an edible ecosystem: a consciously designed community of mutually beneficial plants and animals intended for human food production. Edible forest gardens can provide more than just a wide variety of foodstuffs; the seven F's apply here: food, fuel, fiber, fodder (food for animals), fertilizer, and "farmaceuticals," as well as fun. A beautiful, lush environment is either a conscious focus of the garden design, or a side-benefit one enjoys.

The forest garden mimics forest ecosystems, those naturally occurring perennial polycultures originally found throughout the humid climates of the world. In much of North America, your garden would soon begin to revert to forest if you were to stop tilling and weeding it. Annual and perennial weeds would first colonize the bare soil. In a few years, shrubs would follow the weeds as the dominant plants. Finally, the pioneer trees would move in, and a forest would be born. It can take many decades for this process, called succession, to result in a mature forest.

We humans work hard to hold back succession—mowing, weeding, plowing, spraying. If the successional process were the wind, we would be constantly motoring against it. Why not put up a sail and glide along with the land's natural tendency to become forest? Edible forest gardening is about expanding the horizons of our food gardening across the full range of the successional sequence, from field to forest, and everything in between.[6]

Permaculture

David Holmgren, one of the founders of permaculture, has this to say about it.

The word permaculture was coined by Bill Mollison and myself in the mid-1970's to describe an integrated, evolving system of perennial or self-perpetuating plant and animal species useful to man.[7]

A more current definition of permaculture, which reflects the expansion of focus implicit in Permaculture One, is "Consciously designed landscapes which mimic the patterns and relationships found in nature, while yielding an abundance of food, fibre and energy for provision of local needs." People, their buildings and the ways in which they organize themselves are central to permaculture. Thus the permaculture vision of permanent or sustainable agriculture has evolved to one of permanent or sustainable culture.

126

For many people, myself included, the above conception of permaculture is so global in its scope that its usefulness is reduced. More precisely, I see permaculture as the use of systems thinking and design principles that provide the organizing framework for implementing the above vision. It draws together the diverse ideas, skills and ways of living which need to be rediscovered and developed in order to empower us to provide for our needs, while increasing the natural capital for future generations.

In this more limited but important sense, permaculture is not the landscape, or even the skills of organic gardening, sustainable farming, energy efficient building or eco-village development as such, but it can be used to design, establish, manage and improve these and all other efforts made by individuals, households and communities towards a sustainable future.[8]

The Worldwide Permaculture Network links permaculture project and people around the globe. At this writing (September 2014) it lists 367 permaculture projects in the USA and 60 in California alone.[9] The accuracy of the directory depends on projects and people around the world to self-report. It misses, therefore, some projects that have not opted to be listed.

One of the most significant permaculture projects in Sonoma County is not listed in the directory. The Permaculture Skills Center in Sebastopol has a nine-month residential training program and Taproot Farm, which offers a Community Supported Agriculture program. They are pioneering with a Community-Grown Agriculture program that enlists volunteers who exchange labor and learning for discounts on the farm's produce. The Permaculture Skills Center is a well-organized and well-run program with excellent community involvement and support.

Community Supported Agriculture

Community Supported Agriculture consists of a community of individuals who pledge support to a farm operation so that the farmland becomes, either legally or spiritually, the community's farm, with the growers and consumers providing mutual support and sharing the risks and benefits of food production. Typically, members or "share-holders" of the farm or garden pledge in advance to cover the anticipated costs of the farm operation and farmer's salary. In return, they receive shares in the farm's bounty throughout the growing season, as well as satisfaction gained from reconnecting to the land and participating directly in food production. Members also share in the risks of farming, including poor harvests due to unfavorable weather or pests. By direct sales to community members, who have provided the farmer with working capital in advance, growers receive better prices for their crops, gain some financial security, and are relieved of much of the burden of marketing.[10]

You can find a CSA near you with the help of the web page of Local Harvest, Real Food, Real Farmers, Real Community.[11]

Locavore Movement

The locavore movement is a relatively recent creation. The movement consists of people who have decided that it is better to eat food grown or gathered within 100 or so miles of where they live. The word *locavore* is first reported to have been heard in 2005. In 2007 it was named Word of the Year by the Oxford American Dictionary. That gives some idea about how fast the movement has been spreading.[12]

A locavore here on the California coast might eat very much like the Miwok Indians who once inhabited this part of the world.

There was a big variety of food available for the Coast and Lake Miwok. Acorns were one of their basic foods. Nuts from the yellow and sugar pine trees as well as the seeds that came from the pine cones were eaten. Berries from the California laurel tree were made into cakes, or to make a drink something like chocolate. Dried manzanita berries were ground into a flour that was rolled into balls and eaten as a sweet. Then as now, the sea was an important source of food. Miwoks ate fish, eels, crabs, mussels, and clams. Seaweed was gathered and dried. Trout and other freshwater fish were caught from streams. Salmon were easily taken as they came up the rivers and streams to spawn. Deer and elk were hunted all year. Deer bones were cracked open to get the marrow. Smaller animals such as rabbits, squirrels, wood rats, and gophers were easier to catch, and birds were hunted for food and feathers. Ducks, geese, mud hens, and other waterfowl, as well as quail and other land birds, were caught in traps or nets.[13]

It is hard to realize now after the whole area has been civilized and the fossil fuel economy has dominated the ecology that before 1849 California coastal hills supported abundant herds of elk and deer, streams and lakes were filled with fish, and the forests had not been clear-cut. There is a woodcut picture with a view of Santa Barbara from the sea in the 1850s that shows the hills above it on fire. The local band of the Chumash nurtured herds of elk and deer by burning off the golden hills of summer so more abundant fresh grass would grow during the rainy season.

Contemporary locavores are dependent on farmers, ranchers, dairy keepers, and fishermen and women to fill their larders. It is very easy to eat well in Sonoma County on only those foods grown or gathered within 100 miles. For those of you living in big cities it might be a bit more difficult.

We have two neighbors here in the Estero Americano Valley who are dedicated to sustainable agriculture and run very successful CSAs as well as marketing their produce in local farm markets.

Mike Collins of Bloomfield Organics has worked the soil for 37 years. In addition to growing organic vegetables, strawberries, eggs, and herbs, Mike has a vision for the future. He hopes we can build a self-sustaining economy in the Estero Valley. He states the mission for Bloomfield Organics this way.

> It is our mission at Bloomfield Organics to grow certified organic and heirloom produce of unparalleled nutrition, freshness, and quality. We strive to be the reliable sustainable farming "partner of choice" to our customers and suppliers, all the while taking great care to conserve and regenerate the lands we steward in the Estero Americano Watershed.

Guido Fasini is the fourth generation of his family to run the farm on their land in the Estero Valley.

> This land has been in my family since 1867 and it's that same test of time that now lies at the heart of what we do here at True Grass Farms. We've since expanded the scope of that legacy, reaching beyond just four generations to inherit an even older wisdom: By nurturing unique natural cycles, we in turn are nurtured by the land—an understanding that reveals itself in the quality of our products as well as in the sustainability of our operation.
>
> For us, it all begins with the grass. We commit ourselves to maintaining healthy pastureland by embracing a process of rotational grazing that depends upon the stewardship of a natural ecosystem—of which we as well as the grass are only two elements. Here we raise Black Angus cows and California Kobe, a Japanese breed, renowned for their flavor and tenderness, along with American Guinea and Blackworth hogs, rabbit and heritage chicken breeds. Tucked within the coastal valleys of Marin County, we strive toward a more harmonious relationship with our environment so as to provide the best local source of fine beef, pork and other pasture-raised USDA-certified organic meats to our community.

Both Fasini and Collins recognize that their success depends on a whole network, a community of not just producers in sustainable agriculture, but of the people who support their CSAs by committing to buy its products, by the workers

130

and volunteers participate in it and probably, most importantly by those who live nearby and have deep appreciation for
what their neighbors and friends are doing.

Next we move on to methods and means to develop and
organize small communities based on the memes of the new
humanity.

---

[1] beehivecollective.org/en/

[2] Ariana Strozzi, *Horse Sense for the Leader Within: Expanded
Edition: An Equine Guided Approach to Self Leadership,*
CreateSpace Independent Publishing Platform, 2011.

[3] Michael Pollan, "The Intelligent Plant: Scientists debate a new way
of understanding flora," *The New Yorker,* December 23, 2013.

[4] "So it's unsettling (but also the first unambiguously good news
this book has to offer) to learn that serious people have begun
to rethink small-scale agriculture, perhaps just in time to help us
deal with the strains of our new planet. In the last ten years
academics and researchers have begun figuring out what some
farmers have known for a long time: It's possible to produce lots
of food on relatively small farms with little or nothing in the way
of synthetic fertilizer or chemicals."—Bill McKibben, *Eaarth:
Making a Life on a Tough New Planet,* Henry Holt and Co.,
Kindle Edition, 2010, p. 166.

[5] The National Sustainable Agriculture Information Service—
ATTRA—is developed and managed by the National Center for
Appropriate Technology (NCAT). Visit the NCAT website for
more information on sustainable agriculture and energy projects:
https://attra.ncat.org/index.php

[6] David Jacke, *Edible Forest Gardens: A Delicious and Practical
Ecology,* Chelsea Green Publishing, 2005.

[7] Bill Mollison and David Holmgren, *Permaculture One: A
Perennial Agriculture for Human Settlements,* International Tree
Crop Institute USA, 1981.

[8] *The Essence of Permaculture*,
http://holmgren.com.au/downloads/Essence_of_Pc_EN.pdf

[9] http://www.permacultureglobal.com

[10] From the National Agricultural Library of the US Department of Agriculture,
http://www.nal.usda.gov/afsic/pubs/csa/csa.shtml#find

[11] http://www.localharvest.org

[12] Laughing Planet Café, http://www.planetmattersandmore.com

[13] Social Studies Fact Cards,
http://factcards.califa.org/cai/miwokcoastandlake.html

Chapter 13

Communities

With many others we'll help build the architecture for the world that comes next, the dispersed and localized societies that can survive the damage we can no longer prevent. Eaarth represents the deepest of human failures. But we still must live on the world we've created lightly, carefully, gracefully.

—*Bill McKibben*[1]

THE SINGLE MOST IMPORTANT thing for those of us who want to create a new humanity during the time of the apocalypse and in the time that follows is that we cannot do it alone. We need to build communities that are based on the new memes of love and trust. We have assumed that the hierarchical model of community life was divinely inspired when in fact it was a manifestation of the domination/violence system of civilization. The gods did not ordain the domination/violence system. The domination/violence system fabricated the gods to justify and validate its iniquities. Now as civilization is dying around us, so are both the gods and the hierarchical model of community and organizational life.

Our task is to discover new memes and create new processes for communities based on love and trust. How can we structure communities where love and trust are primary?

The answers to those questions can be found in our recent history. In Chapter 12 we saw that there are a number of organizations and systems that are already creating new ways to replace fossil fuel-based, industrialized agriculture that are more respectful of the natural environment. Likewise, many of the clues to shaping new communities based on love and trust can be found in the work of people in the last century who were disabused of the hierarchical model of organizational life. (You may recall my discussion of the work of Jack Gibb and his TORI Theory in Chapter 9.)

Before we get to the discussion about the structure and process of new communities for the new humanity, we need to look at one critical and similar element that I have not addressed: wisdom. You know what wisdom is—a combination of knowledge, experience, openness of mind, good judgment, patience, and wholeness.

The machinations of political leaders in the Washington Beltway after 9/11 have demonstrated that when domination and violence are the principal values, wisdom tends to go out the window and stupid mistakes are made over and over again. When the solution to every crisis is a military action, the domination/violence solution, wisdom is undeniably absent from every policy consideration. The Commander-in-Chief,[2] under the influence of his domination-addicted advisors in the military, the State Department, the CIA, and the Department of Homeland Security, is now totally devoid of his personal wisdom and he has no wise advisors.

We need to reframe the question. It is now "What is the structure and process in communities where love, trust, *and* wisdom are primary?"

One thing is certain. Communities that are structured to enhance love, trust, and wisdom are not hierarchical. In hierarchical organizations power is concentrated at the top and there are structured sets of behaviors or roles for leaders and for the follower.

Leader	Follower
Power	Submission
Control	Obedience
Authority	Dependence
Assures Security	Fealty
Knowledge	Ignorance
Has Security	Seeks Security
Dispenses Rewards	Seeks Approval

If the leader's benefice is not appreciated, the followers are blamed and shamed. If the followers are not secure in their fealty, the leader is blamed and shamed. In both instances mistrust and enmity are generated. Everyone is restive and unhappy.

In hierarchical systems some power is dispensed downward to retainers. The same sets of behavior prevail between retainers and followers and the result is more mistrust and enmity.

Communities structured as hierarchical systems do not generate relationships of love, trust and wisdom. The widespread social and political dis-ease in countries around the world today is sufficient evidence of that truth.

Because of the memes that accompany a hierarchical structure, hierarchies tend to grow larger and larger with more and more power at the top. That is another description of the disease that is now destroying civilization from within.

The shape of a community in which the memes of love and trust and wisdom prevail is a circle, not a triangle. In a circle power is not concentrated in one place, but distributed evenly to all the members of the circle.

I discovered the power and wisdom of circles in the early 60s when I became fascinated with Amerindian spirituality and culture. For several years one of my major recreations was reading about and immersing myself in as much Amerindian culture as possible. I share the common tendency to affirm our cultural self-interests by reshaping what we observe of other cultures and other times. What I learned about Amerindian culture and thought had the opposite effect on me. It forced me to question how I knew what I knew. I had a metanoia experience, an epistemological crisis and conversion. I was changed by what I read and what I observed.[3]

Black Elk tells about his Oglala Sioux culture.

> You have noticed that everything an Indian does is in a circle, and that is because the Power of the World always works in circles, and everything tries to be round.

> In the old days when we were a strong and happy people, all our power came to us from the sacred hoop of the nation, and so long as the hoop was unbroken, the people flourished. The flowering tree was the living center of the hoop, and the circle of the four quarters nourished it.

> The east gave peace and light, the south gave warmth, the west gave rain, and the north with its cold and mighty wind gave strength and endurance.

> This knowledge came to us from the outer world with our religion. Everything the Power of the World does is done in a circle.

> The sky is round, and I have heard that the earth is round like a ball, and so are all the stars.

> The wind, in its greatest power, whirls.

> Birds make their nests in circles, for theirs is the same religion as ours.

The sun comes forth and goes down again in a circle. The moon does the same, and both are round.

Even the seasons form a great circle in their changing, and always come back again to where they were.

The life of a man is a circle from childhood to childhood, and so it is in everything where power moves.

Our tepees were round like the nests of birds, and these were always set in a circle, the nation's hoop, a nest of many nests, where the Great Spirit meant for us to hatch our children.[4]

Amerindians believed that knowledge and wisdom was the product of the input of every member of the community. Each of us comes from a unique place in life—unique talents, skills, insights, experiences—and each is at a different stage of maturity and growth. Each person sits in a different place on the circle of life, bringing his or her own perspective to the circle. Each sees the object (or subject) in the center of the circle in a unique way. Hyemeyohsts Storm in *Seven Arrows*[5] says that the true nature of an object is only clear when every person's perspective is heard and honored. A simple thing like a stone looks different from every point on the circle. Looking at an idea is much more complex.

Reading about Council Circles was even more significant for me. I vividly remember Gene Weltfish's account of the Pawnee Council Circle planning their winter buffalo hunt.[6] A representative of each family sat in the circle around a fire and each in turn, sunwise around the circle, spoke whatever was on his or her mind—a recollection, a fable, a dream, a vision, a feeling. Around and around the circle, the offerings were made as if to the fire in the center. After a time, the council circle ended, and the next day everyone in the village knew their task and did it. No arguments had been presented; no motions had been made and seconded; no votes taken.

The planning had been done, the jobs assigned, and the preparations completed. It happened as the result of sharing the wisdom.

So I began to experiment with circles. I asked groups of friends and colleagues to help me stage circle experiences. I gave them some guidance about what we were going to do. I placed a simple array of objects in the center of the circle. I asked each person sunwise (clockwise) around the circle to say whatever he or she wished about that array—dreams, fantasies, ideas, descriptions, whatever. Our objective was to understand the meaning and spiritual significance of the array. Time after time, we were moved by the spiritual dimension of the event, the beauty and wisdom that emerged.

In hierarchical groups in the domination culture, two or three self-assured leaders dominate a dialogic discussion, and other people who are introverted or less self-assured are subservient players, silent for the most part. In the circle process all voices have equal weight and equal authority.

In the sixties and seventies when part of my work was in organizational development consulting, I began to use the circle way for organizational decision-making and conflict resolution. I was searching for a way out of the traditional kinds of organization that are based on a hierarchical, conflict-oriented model of domination systems. I wanted something other than the parliamentary procedures set out in Robert's Rules of Order or the dialogic pattern of polarized argumentation. As Deborah Tannen puts it,

> Our determination to pursue truth by setting up a fight between two sides leads us to believe that every issue has two sides—no more, no less: If both sides are given a forum to confront each other, all the relevant information will emerge, and the best case will be made for each side. But opposition does not lead to truth when an issue is not composed of two

opposing sides but is a crystal of many sides. Often the truth is in the complex middle, not the oversimplified extremes.[7]

I worked with a number of different organizations to do such things as consider and adopt a budget, consider and adopt program goals and strategies, and enhance organizational effectiveness.

The process was simple. After stating the issue at hand, we would go around the circle sunwise until we reached a consensual decision. Our contract was that the wisdom of the whole group would emerge if we trusted the process and offered to the center our best gifts, whether those were dreams, fantasies, ideas, feelings, or convictions. Note: It is very important to emphasize that the wisdom of the group depends on the expression of all our gifts, including honest revelations of our wildness, our hostilities, and our shadow sides.

Always the consensus just seemed to emerge. We all knew it without asking a question like, "Have we reached a consensus?" The circle method may take more time, but the result is that good decisions are made, everyone has input, and no one is overridden or outvoted. When the process ends no one is nursing leftover bad feelings. Organizational conflict becomes a memory. And, most surprisingly, when we set a time to adjourn the meeting before we started the circle, we completed our business in the time allotted without feeling pressured.

Although I was not aware of it at the time, many others had begun to experiment with the circles. Their experiments emerged from their work as therapists, educators, counselors, and personal-growth trainers. Some introduced circles in schools, nonprofits, and businesses. They report outstanding success wherever they have applied the method. Among those exploring the new way to be human are:

- **Christina Baldwin** is a circle-way pioneer. She published what may be the primary book in the field, *Calling the Circle: The First and Future Culture.* She dramatically presents the centrality of circles in Amerindian and other premodern cultures. Baldwin's sense of the future culture is, I think, compromised by her notion that hierarchical systems and peer systems like circles can complement one another in the same institutions. I think she vastly underrates the coercive power of a domination system and the violence that sustains it.

- **Jean Shinoda Bolen,** the well-known and widely read Jungian therapist, wrote a poetic small book called *The Millionth Circle: How to Change Ourselves and the World,* in which she proposes ". . . nothing less than the visionary possibility that women's circles can accelerate humanity's shift to a post-patriarchal era." Except for the fact that she leaves men totally out of the process, it is a powerful little book.

- **Cecile Andrews,** in *The Circle of Simplicity: Return to the Good Life,* writes an eloquent description of her experience with circles of people across the nation who are seeking to live more simply. Cecile and her cohorts are experiencing the rebirth of a phenomenon that began centuries ago and is being rediscovered.

We don't need to depend on experts, teachers, politicians, gurus, priests, or clergy to lead us. Circles are not hierarchical or patriarchal. Circles honor the truth that wisdom is discovered as a gift that comes when the offering of each person is given and received with thanksgiving. Because we can go around and around the circle until we discover the hidden depths, circles are a healing, forgiving process that release us from the oppression of one-upmanship into an empowering

140

freedom that is a life-affirming process of support and comfort.

We are living in the last days of the domination/violence system, which manifests as the hierarchical/patriarchal structure in groups and systems. We need to die to the memes that support the dying hierarchies and replace them with the love, trust, and wisdom of the circle structure and process. Beginning to use the circle process now in all our organizations is the prefigurative way toward a post-civilized human being during the apocalypse and beyond.

In the next chapter we will describe how the circle process works.

---

[1] Bill McKibben, *Eaarth: Making a Life on a Tough New Planet,* Henry Holt and Co., Kindle Edition, p. 212.

[2] Commander-in-Chief is now the default title for the President of the United States, designating him as the dominator in chief.

[3] The following section is based on material I developed in my book, *JESUS CIRCLES: A Way to Heal Our Wounds, Subvert the Domination System, and Build an Abundant Future,* Xlibris, 2004.

[4] Nicholas Black Elk, *Black Elk Speaks: Being the Life Story of a Holy Man of the Oglala Sioux,* as told through John G. Neihardt (Flaming Rainbow), Electronic Edition published by the University of Nebraska Press at http://www.blackelkspeaks.unl.edu/toc.htm, p. 150.

[5] Hyemeyohsts Storm, *Seven Arrows,* Ballantine Books, 1985.

[6] Gene Weltfish, *The Lost Universe: Pawnee Life and Culture,* University of Nebraska Press, reissue edition, 1990.

[7] Deborah Tannen, *The Argument Culture: Stopping America's War of Words,* third paper edition, Ballantine Books, 1999, p. 3.

Chapter 14

The circle process

*Our Teachers tell us that all things within this Universe
Wheel know of their harmony with every other thing,
and know how to **Give-Away**, one to the other, except
man. Of all the Universe's creatures, it is we alone who
do not begin our lives with knowledge of this great
Harmony.*

*All the things of the Universe Wheel have spirit and life,
including the rivers, rocks, earth, sky, plants and
animals. But it is only man of all the Beings on the
Wheel, who is a determiner. Our determining spirit can
be made whole only through the learning of our
harmony with all our brothers and sisters, and with all
the other spirits of the Universe. To do this you must learn
to seek and to perceive. We must do this to find our place
within the Medicine Wheel. To determine this place we
must learn to **Give-Away**.*[1]

BECAUSE THEY ARE SO PREDOMINANT in our domina-
tion/violence culture, I assume that you are involved in at
least a few hierarchical groups and organizations. Unfortunately for some of you, one of these may be your family. It
may be your workplace, your church, or your local political

party. This chapter may help you to turn one of your hierarchical groups into a small community where love, trust, and wisdom prevail.

You may not be the designated leader of the group, but as a member of it you have all the potential to be a leader, because leadership is not a role, it is a cluster of functions. Helping group members to communicate better is one leadership function. You can help the group to be more effective at the same time you are helping it to become prefigurative of the next evolutionary stage of humanity.

Pick the group you want to help. The next time it meets, exercise your leadership. Appoint yourself the convener. Take the bull by the horns by suggesting that the group try a new process, "just this time to see how it works." You can explain how the process maximizes the talents or gifts of everyone in the room, gives everyone a chance to contribute, and has the best possibility of making good decisions.

Before anyone has a chance to object you say,

"I want us to try the circle process. We go around the circle (or table, if that's where you are) to the left each person speaking, one at a time, saying whatever it is they want to say. When you are through talking, simply let the person on your left know that you are through. If you choose not to speak you may simply say 'pass.' We should have no cross-talk; you have to wait for your turn to speak. I will start. Each of us finishes the sentence 'Right now I am feeling . . .'"

"I am feeling apprehensive and hopeful at the same time." Indicate that you are through by signaling to the person on your left.

You will probably feel like a fledgling bird taking flight for the first time. You are indeed flying and you are relying on your inherent sense of trust that it will work and people will find it enjoyable.

It may be necessary in a group that is not accustomed to the process to cut someone off who speaks out of turn by saying, "Please, no crosstalk. Wait for your turn."

When a group has become accustomed to the circle process, the ritual is internalized and it flows naturally and easily with little need for process interventions from a convener.

What follows is a more elaborate explanation of rituals[2] of the circle process and suggestions about making it more effective.

1. Gathering

When a group gathers there is usually an exchange of pleasantries, introductions, and re-connections. Then everyone takes a seat in a circle of chairs. The most effective groups actually sit in chairs facing the center, not around a rectangular table. The order in which people are seated doesn't matter at all. As happens in all groups over time, eventually everyone will take the same seat, the one that feels most comfortable.

2. Silence and centering

It is good to have a brief period of silence and centering, a time to let go of the anxieties, noise, and distractions we usually carry with us through the day. There may be a guided centering exercise like a gentle reminder that following and watching one's breathing is perhaps the simplest centering method.

In a novice or stranger group I have frequently used a "safety check." I ask the members of the group to check their bodies to see if they feel any discomfort or pain that will keep them from being totally present here and now. I ask them to look around the room and check to see if they feel safe and secure in this place. Finally, I ask them to look at each person in the circle to see if they feel comfortable with these people. On the very, very rare occasion when someone says they don't feel safe or comfortable, I ask them to take a moment to do something about their discomfort. Sometimes a suggestion that the discomfort be put aside for the time being will work. Usually the problem can be easily solved, and we can go to the next step.

3. Check-in sunwise

Check-in is always the next step. Members respond to questions like these:

- Can you tell us how it's been for you since the last time we were together?

- Can you tell us what's happened in your life since our last meeting?[3]

The responses always move from one person to the next sunwise (clockwise—to the left) around the circle. It is very important to make clear that it is *always* acceptable to pass and let the next person on the left speak.

One way to tell the person on your left that you are finished with your contribution is to lightly touch that person. Some groups prefer the use of a "talking stick" that is passed from one person to the next. The stick may be very simple or it may be ceremonially decorated. The virtue of a talking stick is that it indicates that only the person holding the stick may talk.

A touch or a passed talking stick also enables a "pass." Somehow, given our culturally infused sense of inadequacy, it seems embarrassing to have to say, "I pass." Given our sense of built-in unworthiness, that's too often felt as "I'm a dummy and I have nothing to add." Or "I am too stupid about this whole subject."

4. Identify the topic for the session or the issue to be resolved and the agreed time for ending

It may be that the circle has a preset issue or topic to address, such as determining how to respond to a call for a demonstration against some political policy. Or it may be that the circle is the board of a local water association that must deal with delinquent accounts. The specific task or agenda should be noted and addressed following check-in. When appropriate the time for adjournment is also stated.

5. Offer your gift to the center of the circle

A very important ritual is that all contributions are made to the center of the circle. It is as though I am offering my report, my thought, my fantasy, my dream, this part of my wisdom to all of you by placing it in the center of our circle as a gift to all. Any kind of comment is acceptable and offered without embarrassment, self-consciousness, or judgment.

Offering one's wisdom or insight to the center of the circle is a collaborative act. It recognizes that each individual's wisdom is very limited and the whole wisdom is the exponential sum of all our unique wisdoms. You are not addressing one person in the circle; your offering is to all. (See endnote on eye contact.[4])

6. No cross talk

Another ritual of the circle process is that there is no cross talk. It makes no difference how much I need to respond to your comment. I have to wait for my turn in the circle. Your statement was made to the group as a whole, and I am only one member of the group, even if you seem to have made a specific criticism of me or my point of view.

Deborah Tannen has campaigned against "a pervasive warlike atmosphere that makes us approach public dialogue, and just about anything we need to accomplish, as if it were a fight." She writes:

> It [the adversarial frame of mind, Ed.] is a tendency in Western culture in general, and in the United States in particular, that has a long history and a deep, thick, and far-ranging root system. It has served us well in many ways but in recent years has become so exaggerated that it is getting in the way of solving our problems. Our spirits are corroded by living in an atmosphere of unrelenting contention—an argument culture.
>
> The argument culture urges us to regard the world—and the people in it—in an adversarial frame of mind. It rests on the assumption that opposition is the best way to get anything done: The best way to explore an idea is to set up a debate; the best way to cover the news is to find spokespeople who express the most extreme, polarized views and present them as "both sides"; the best way to settle disputes is litigation that pits one party against the other; the best way to begin an essay is to oppose someone; and the best way to show you're really thinking is to criticize and attack. The war on drugs, the war on cancer, the battle of the sexes, politicians' turf battles—in the argument culture, war metaphors pervade our talk and shape our thinking.[5]

We can easily substitute "domination-system culture" for her term "argument culture." Metaphors of war and violence permeate our sports, films, television, and daily discourse. The circle process is one way to get the wisdom that can lead us to the just and nonviolent domain of post-civilized new humanity.

It is very difficult to have an argument with another member of the circle when each person must take his or her turn in order, and there is no cross talk. What tends to happen is that an interpersonal issue has faded away by the time it's my turn to respond to what I heard as a hostile statement. New data, new feelings, new thoughts have intervened, and the energy has shifted away from conflict and toward shared wisdom. So, no cross talk.

The act of real listening is an act of love, the more so when it may be absorbing the anger, defensiveness, and hostility of another.

7. Confidentiality—what's said in this group stays in this group

Because the effectiveness of the circle process depends upon loving mutual trust and the freedom to speak with utmost honesty, it is essential to agree to strict confidentiality among members of the group. We make an agreement to keep what is said in this circle in this group and not speak of it or mention it to others outside of our group.

I experienced this violation of the confidentiality principle one day many years ago. This is a slightly fictionalized account to protect the guilty. A friend had confided in me that he was a member of an Addicts Anonymous Group. Months later, as we were working together, he casually asked me if I knew the Reverend So-and-So. Whoops! I not only knew him, he had once been my boss. I answered by saying no more than "yes," but my friend blurted out, "I shouldn't have said that." He had broken trust with his peers in his recovery group. I had suspected that my former boss was abusing drugs but had no real data to support my guess. Now I knew and should not have learned it this way.

8. An ending ritual

Ending any kind of a group meeting means that relationships are partially severed; a passage is made to a new set of relationships, a new time of life. In one sense we bury one part of our lives to be born again in another. *Goodbye* is a contraction that really means, "God by ye." That is, "God be with you while we are apart." It is as though we say, "In this group we have known safety, comfort, love, acceptance, and it is good. Now there is a more cruel and precarious world into which we must move, and I want you to be safe, comfortable, loved, accepted, and have it all be good."

The ending of a circle shouldn't be like that awful period of anticipated separation between a teenager and parent. The parent says, "I love this kid and the kid loves me, and his/her impending departure for college or some other distant place is going to be really hard on me." The kid is saying, "I don't want to leave home, but I have to, or I'll never grow up. I love my mom and dad, and I don't know how I'll be able to get along without them, but I have to. God, I hate this."

In order to spare themselves the heartbreak of separation, both parents and kids become silent and withdrawn, angry and hateful toward one another. To help them separate, they need to feign disgust with one another. Both parents and the kid are pretending, "What a relief to be rid of you."

The same sort of undermining phenomenon can occur when people in less intimate relationships separate. To assuage our dismay when we are ending a group meeting, we tend to discount what we mean to each other. Structuring a ritual time for separation is, therefore, very important to the continuing health of the group and its members.

When the time comes to end a circle session, you have a number of options.

- You may do one more round, asking for final comments like "What this session has meant to me," or "What I have received during this session," or "I am thankful for this evening because . . ."

- You may do a final round in which each person makes an action commitment like "What I will do this week to undermine the domination system," or "What I will do this week to be what I want the world to be."

- In a spiritually based group, a final round might end with each member saying a prayer for the person on his/her left. (Reaching out and touching them at the same time.)

When a group has become accustomed to the circle process, the ritual is internalized and it flows naturally and easily with little need for process interventions from a convener.

In the next chapter we will look at the four critical factors in the dynamics of group life.

---

[1] Hyemeyohsts Storm, *Seven Arrows,* Ballantine Books, New York, 1972.

[2] A series of actions or type of behavior regularly and invariably followed by someone (*New Oxford American Dictionary*).

[3] The renowned family therapist Virginia Satir rarely asked a direct question of her clients. She always framed her question with, "Can you tell me about . . ." or "Is it possible for you to tell me about . . .?" This allows the respondent to say, if they choose, "No, I can't tell you about that." Usually, however, any defensiveness is dissipated by the permissive way the inquiry is framed.

[4] "Make and keep eye contact" is the advice usually given in training sessions for public speakers, managers, and leaders. That's good advice if you are addressing a crowd of hundreds seated in an auditorium or classroom. It is good advice for anyone trying to make their way in a domination system because it is the way predators behave. Predators chase and kill. They have eyes in the front of their skulls, the better to see their prey. Prey animals have eyes on the side of their skulls, the better to be on the lookout for predators.

We humans are predators and predation is at the root of the domination/violence system. Strong eye contact shows our power against or over the other. Downcast eyes and the side of the neck exposed to the other are signs of submission and surrender. This is not true with lovers. When they gaze deeply into one another's eyes in adoration, worship, and desire, eye contact is the sharing of souls.

[5] Deborah Tannen, *The Argument Culture: Stopping America's War of Words,* Ballantine Books, 1999, p. 10.

Chapter 15

Understanding group process

Jesus was right about one thing: Any group larger than 12 is doomed.

—*E. F. Schumacher*[1]

ONE THEME HAS BEEN CENTRAL to me for almost as long as I can remember. I have tried to figure out how to help make people's lives better. That involves how to understand what's going on in me, what's going on in you, and what's going on between us. It has energized my interest in sociology and clinical psychology. More to the point here, it has motivated my interest in discovering what goes on in groups.

I was fortunate to have found help along the way. In my 20s, I did graduate study in sociology and was invited to attend a weeklong Group Life Laboratory training session sponsored and paid for by the Episcopal Church. Group Life Labs were a training process developed by the National Training Laboratory[2] (NTL), which had been founded by Kurt Lewin. That was my first exposure to understanding the dynamics of life in groups and foundational for the rest of my career both in and outside of the church.

Several years later I was invited to attend a weeklong Community Development Laboratory that had also been developed by NTL. That gave me another major bump in understanding and working with community organization and growth. At about the same time I met William Pfeiffer, a pioneer in Organizational Development consulting. He had been on the faculty of Iowa State University and with his colleague, John Jones, had organized University Associates, a vehicle for bringing Organizational Development resources to business, industry, and nonprofits. I became a part-time Associate and worked with other members of University Associates to do training and consulting around the country. In the 1970s after a two-year stint working as a political staffer in an Indiana gubernatorial campaign, I morphed into a full-time organizational consultant and Effectiveness Training Instructor.[3]

As I learned about group dynamics and process on the ground, I also read widely and discovered a host of theories about group life. The problem for me was that each of the theoretical models related to only one aspect of the process. One model, for example, described the issues around incorporating new members into a group, another about dealing with the loss of a member, another about maximizing member participation. Partly in frustration and partly out of curiosity, I tried to develop a model that integrated all the aspects of group life.

The memes of industrialized civilization cause us to think of communities and organizations as structures that are linear and have characteristics similar to a production line. You put people in here, directions and tools in there, line them up and they produce goods, services, and more importantly, profits. The memes of industrialized civilization are wrong. Communities, organizations, and groups are really organisms; they are born/created, they grow and change, they wither and die.

Now to the Cat-Pad.

One day I was making a presentation on group life to faculty and students at the Indiana School of Medicine in Indianapolis. I drew the diagram below on a flip chart, explaining it as I went along. At the end of my presentation I opened up for questions. A member of the faculty, one of the first respondents, said he had a comment and not a question. "You ought to call it the Cat-Pad. If you don't pay attention to the cat, it will mess up the entire pad."

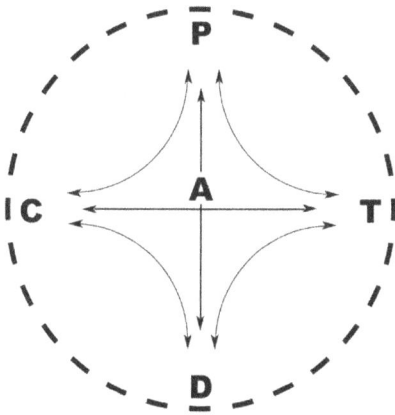

The dotted line around the perimeter of the diagram represents the semipermeable boundary of the group's life. The boundary determines what is inside and what is outside of the group. Every group, organization, or system is embedded in and influenced by the forces and factors of its natural and social environment.

Four basic factors operate in the ongoing life of a group or system.

P = the People who are "members"; i.e., those who function as part of the team or group. People move in and out or their life situations change.

C = the Controls consist of the rules, customs, norms, the "way we do things" that order the group's process. The rules may have to change as a result of new laws or regulations, or the repeal of the same.

D = the Data, all the facts, information, and knowledge that the group uses in its life and work. New information, discoveries, or processes may precipitate changes for the group.

T = the Task, purpose, or objective that defines the group and connects it to a larger system. A shifting market or a new opportunity for action may change the group's task.

Because groups are organisms, any change in or of the People involved will cause the group to examine and perhaps make changes in their Controls, their Task, or their Data. Likewise, any new information or Data will precipitate an examination and perhaps changes in the People involved, Controls, and the Task. No matter which of the four factors changes, it does affect the other three. Much like any natural organism, the group is in a constant state of ebb and flow, seeking to find a healthier equilibrium.

When a group is able to accept, understand, and participate in the process of change and do so with ease and grace, they the members experience a very positive, high affect (A). Everyone feels good, powerful, effective, and satisfied. It is what Jack Gibb called high Q, high quality.

When members of a group are unable or unwilling to deal with that ever-flowing organic dynamic, or their need for stability and security is dominant, the group will be demoralized, everyone will feel bad and they will suffer from low A or low Q.

As an exercise in better understanding of the Cat-Pad I want to introduce you to the White Rock Cooperative. The story of the cooperative is pure fiction. I've written it for your edification. I wish it were true.

As you read this story, think about the changes that the group dealt with over the course of this short recounting of key episodes in its early life together.

When did they need to deal with People changes?

At what points did they have to deal with Control changes?

What Data or new information caused them to change?

What, if anything, precipitated them to change their Task?

The White Rock Cooperative

It began at the University of California in Davis with a small group of undergraduates. Three of them, Archie, Jim, and Evie, were in the College of Agricultural and Environmental Sciences majoring in Sustainable Agriculture and Food Systems. Archie had taken some courses in Animal Science and Management, where he met Will. Will's high school sweetheart, Sue, was majoring in music and through her they met her roommate, Jennifer, who was majoring in Native American studies. They had a natural, easygoing camaraderie and an uncommon taste for afternoon teas. Over time they discovered that each of them had almost the same dream.

The dream was to be part of an alternative, self-sustaining permaculture community living as much as possible off the grid. The more they talked, the more their fantasies took shape about a new kind of living, the more they began to say, "Let's figure out a way to do it." By the end of their junior year they had made a commitment to one another that before they graduated, they would have a workable plan.

One of their first concerns was to find out what kind an organization would most meet their need and yet conform to the California laws about business organizations. After doing research and much discussion they decided to organize a nonprofit cooperative. They named it the UCDC Cooperative.

The next set of decisions focused on economics; not exactly economics, but how they could get the money together to buy a country property they could develop into a residential permaculture community. Their solution was to make a solemn mutual commitment that for three years after graduating each of them was to find a job, making as much money as possible. They agreed to save as much as possible, and put the savings into a co-op bank account. They also committed

157

to live simply, and together sharing as much as possible. The goal was to save money.

By the third year they had added six more members to their co-op. Eight of them were living in their self-described "monastery." During that third year they began to search for property to purchase. They sought the help of Sue's mother, a realtor in Sonoma and Mendocino Counties who had access to the multiple listing services in each county. The search was long and frustrating. They were finding nothing that met their needs. Finally a possibility emerged.

The White Rock Camp Resort had gone into bankruptcy. The 12-acre resort was nestled into a lovely site on a small river in the Six Rivers National Forest. The camp consisted of a central main building and eight seasonal tent cabins, each sleeping four to six people. The main building had a kitchen, a dining hall, laundry facilities, and women and men's bathrooms and showers. There was also a small manager's apartment. The camp was a bit run down and presented the possibility of being the perfect property for them.

For the small group that had begun in their junior year at UC Davis and now had 12 members, things were working. The White Rock Ranch was being auctioned off by the county for delinquent taxes. The co-op withdrew all but $100 from their bank account and prepared to bid. They won the auction and had $4000 left over.

They changed the UCDC Co-op into the White Rock Cooperative and plans were made to begin rehabilitating the resort and gradually moving in. Within a year five members were still working jobs in the economy and seven had moved in and were beginning the process of planting forest and permaculture gardens and raising hogs.

Over the next two years it was possible for the last five original members to move to the farm and the co-op was inviting carefully selected WOOFers and interns to live-work seminars of various lengths.

You can do another exercise that might help to integrate the Cat-Pad as a way of understanding group life. Think about a group you belong to and what has happened in the last month or two of the process and see if you can identify what P, T, D, or C issues made it necessary to consider its consequences in other factors.

The group you choose to analyze may be your family, your church group, your neighborhood association, or your work team. What you need to keep in mind is that the group is an organism with a constant flow of internal processes by which it maintains itself and makes its way in the world in a healthy way.

The only constant in group life is change. When you experience resistance to change or the need for stability and security, you are probably under the influence of the memes of the domination/violence system. One of the ways in which the dominating oligarchs maintain their position is to keep everyone under them in a constant state of uncertainty and insecurity. As I write this in the early fall of 2014, this strategy is egregiously evident in the propaganda about our vulnerability to terrorism in the Mideast.

The creativity and freedom to live in a vital organic community requires a constant process of evolutionary suicide so that we may be liberated from the memes of the domination/violent system and adopt the memes of the new humanity. A vital organic community also needs the full participation of every member, young and old, hale and feeble, male, female, and everyone not described above (note: with the possible exception of psychopaths which is an issue I will deal with in the next chapter).

Now we move on to the issues of leadership and membership in prefigurative, egalitarian communities.

1 Note: Schumacher was only right if your memes about groups are the memes of industrialized civilization. Memes of the new humanity allow for success in larger assemblies, as you will see later.

2 NTL Institute, http://www.ntl.org/inner.asp?id=177&category=2 NTL's vision is people empowered to create just and compassionate organizations and societies in an interdependent world. The mission of the NTL (National Training Laboratories) Institute for Applied Behavioral Science is to advance Applied Behavioral Science (ABS) in the service of social justice, oppression-free societies, and healthy individuals, groups and organizations in the world.

3 Parent Effectiveness Training, Teacher Effectiveness Training, Leader Effectiveness Training. Thomas Gordon, *Parent Effectiveness Training: The Proven Program for Raising Responsible Children,* Harmony; 30th edition, 2000.

Chapter 16

~~Leadership~~/membership in small communities

Be gentle, be truthful, be fearless.

—*Mahatma Gandhi*

IN THE LAST CHAPTER I alluded to the notion that leadership is a series of functions that productively guide process in group life. I also added that the leadership functions can be and often are exercised by those who are not designated leaders of the group. That is quite true for groups that operate under the memes of the domination/violence system, and there has been a significant amount of detailed study about leadership in group life.

(If you would really like to do a serious study the dynamics of leadership and communication in small groups, read *Communication in Small Groups: Theory, Process, and Skills,*[1] which is available both in a hardback edition and online as a Google book.)

I find it interesting that the studies of the dynamics of group life has involved breaking the process down into finite bites. In *Communication in Small Groups* there is a cluster of skills under the heading of "Problem Solving Skills" and the subheading "Task Leadership Skills," which includes the following functions:

Contributing ideas
Seeking ideas
Evaluating ideas
Seeking idea evaluation
Visualizing abstract ideas
Generalizing from specific ideas

(Each of these categories is further defined by a relatively ample paragraph.)

The underlying assumption seems to be that when these functions are identified and understood, a leader who wants to be an effective problem-solving leader in groups can easily replicate them.

The concept reminds me of Taylorism, the popular name for scientific management,[2] which derives in turn from that branch of Newtonian science that seeks to reduce reality to its smallest possible components.

In the 1950s, when I was working as a laborer at the Winchester Repeating Arms Company, scientific management was alive and well as "Time and Motion Study." The TMS department sought to break down each portion of a production process into its smallest components and assist workers to become more effective in their movements and timing. In our department, machinists worked at lathes cutting the rims and primer pockets in rifle and pistol shells, the final steps prior to being fitted with primer caps, powder, and bullets. The machinists were paid "piece rate," meaning that they were paid by the number of shells that they produced during a given shift. One would think that the machinists might be very pleased to increase the speed of their production, but when the TMS guy came around with his stopwatch and clipboard, they were ready. Their tactic was to slow down every motion of their work. That effectively warped the study in their favor. The underdog can always find a way to undermine the top dogs.

Both the TMS department working on machinists and the Director of Advertising in a meeting with his department were caught up in the old memes of the domination/violence system. The memes of leadership after the Industrial Revolution focused on the individual, whether it was the hero on a quest, an adventurous pioneer, or a powerful super-competent man exploring new technologies and building a new business. Emulating the most powerful dominating male shaped the memes about leadership in virtually every area of life.

Once again I want to emphasize the need to commit evolutionary suicide. Dying to the old leadership memes of the era of civilization will enable us to create new memes for the emerging new humanity.

Let us put the ideas and old memes of leadership away altogether and forever. Then we can be free to explore the dynamics of a small community where there are no designated leaders, no chairmen, no CEOs, no presidents or executives.

I hear you ask, "How does such a leaderless community work?"

In an egalitarian community the unique gifts of every single member are valued as contributing to a healthy whole. When the gifts are withheld or denied, the community is diminished. The circle process enables each member to offer his or her unique gifts to the community. The synthesis of those shared gifts leads the group to its next step of growth and development.

In any egalitarian community functional roles are often necessary, and one person designated to fill the role. One person needs, for example, to convene and guide the circle process. For example, someone may need to be designated to convene a sub-circle to specialize in managing community funds. In the circle process, roles are term-limited and the community may determine the limitation. It is wise to adopt the rule that no one person can hold one role for more than one year. There is no reason why some functional roles cannot rotate monthly or quarterly.

There is a good model for this policy in the egalitarian Bruderhof Communities,[3] who choose a president for a one-year term. They hold community meetings to make decisions about the life of the community, and much like the Quakers they seek to know what God is willing for them at the time. If the community cannot come to a consensus about an issue in a timely way, the president is empowered to make a decision and the members agree to abide by it. The strategy is seldom used.

In the early stages of a small group's life, when it is in the process of formation, it may be appropriate for the person who gathered the group to be the convener for a time. When the circle process becomes normative in the group's life, the convener can raise the issue of new a new convener. The circle will decide whether or not it is the proper time and if it is, which person among them should be the new convener and for what term of service.

In my experience of establishing new circle groups, the experience quickly becomes compelling for the participants. The openness, the trust, and the sense of well-being characteristic of the circle process is very attractive to those who have been accustomed to the tension, competitiveness, and negativity in most hierarchical groups.

In Chapter 13 I presented the "Cat-Pad" as a way of understanding the four major factors in the process of group life. The membership [P] keeps changing, sometimes dramatically, when new people enter the group or leave it. Rules and regulations [C] by which it operates are always in a state of flux, sometimes minor and sometimes dramatic. The information [D] that flows among the members of the group or is available from outside the group is always changing, and finally the group's mission or purpose [T] will adapt to its wider environment and its inner wisdom.

It is the responsibility of every person in the group to be attentive to and responsive to the changes that take place in a way that maintains a high quality [Q] or high affect [A], an atmosphere that is pleasant and works well for everybody.

Before I get to exploring the characteristics of a good member, I want to deal with psychologically sick members. This is especially important when a small group or community begins to welcome new members.

Much too often in my years of working with groups and organizations, I have seen how a disastrous erosion of love and trust is caused by pathological behavior of one or more members or newcomers. Pathology is often not easy to detect. Sociopaths often present themselves as healthy and wholesome people. At the same time they are plotting to manipulate the situation to their own often-destructive ends. Psychopaths may not be as devious. In my experience, however, psychopaths are often attractive people who are genuinely needy and evoke in others the desire to be caring and loving. Both pathologies make it nearly impossible for those so afflicted to participate as loving and trusting community members.[4]

They need the attention and care of specialized healing communities and organizations.

I can see only limited ways in which a community can protect itself from pathological people. The first way is to establish a contract in the community to have a year-long period of trial membership or, as it was called in monastic communities, a novitiate. It is a period for testing whether or not the person is called to be a member of the community. The decision to end the trial membership and the relationship between the novice and the community can be made at any time during the year either by the novice or by the community with no judgementalism, no regrets, no guilt or bad feelings.

If a community detects destructive behavior in one of its members and all of the community's best efforts to help and heal fail, I see no other option but to do what many primitive tribes do, which is to shun or send the miscreant off into the wilderness. Some people may object to this solution as cruel and inhumane, but I would argue that the destruction of the community from within is far more costly to many more people.

So what are the desirable qualities of membership in small communities and groups?

We're not looking for sainthood. It is always in short supply. Given the fact that sin is the most widely distributed of all human commodities, we're not going to find perfection. The best we can hope for among all the members is that they are constantly reaching for the kind of values (memes), skills, and talents that make good members. The underlying foundation for membership is a commitment to learning and growth.

What are the qualities/values/memes toward which you want to grow? Obviously only you can answer that question. Let me tell you how I want to grow.

I want to grow in the spirit of love.

I want love to infuse every moment of my waking life, and it wouldn't be so bad if it also shaped my nighttime dreams.

I want to be able to love my family, my extended family and friends, and groups with whom I work more than I do now.

I want to love them more than I love myself so that the community within which I live is more important than me.

I want to be a loving servant of that community.

I want to grow in compassion and be sensitive to the hurts and needs of the people, the animals, the creepy crawlies, and even the plants in my environment.

I want to grow in generosity, giving more than I receive, expending more than I take in.

I want to grow into a deeper awareness of the wholeness and holiness of all of existence.

I want that wholeness and holiness to supersede and yet comprehend what I perceive as the negative as well as the positive, the conflicting as well as harmonizing forces in the community and in the world.

I want to honor and worship holism and the ultimate mystery, the Tao.

I want to be able to better discern and learn from your feelings, your emotions, and my own. I want to know the richness and complexity, the delight in the disaster in your experience and my own.

I want to know more about your sense of wonder and awe and my own.

I want to be more aware of your imagination and creativity, your wildness and craziness, and my own.

I want to be more deeply aware, more fully cognizant of my shortcomings and limitations, my ignorance and stupidity, my failures and fears, and I want to be more accepting of yours.

I want to be wholly present, here now, awake and attentive with a sense of inner tranquility, inner confidence, and peace.

Finally, I want to be so loving and so trusting as to be fearless in the face of every threat.

Many years ago, before greed became a favored meme among the business community, a high-level CEO I much admired told me that his job was like that of the helmsman or the pilot of a sailing vessel. The helmsman is expected to know the capabilities of his vessel, the shape of its hull, the set of its sails, to be aware of and responsive to the wind and current, the shoals and channels, the capability of his crew, and with steady calm guide the vessel through to its destination.[5]

Learning to be a member is for me like learning to be a spiritually centered helmsman.

If you join or gather a small community that is ready to grow into the kind of membership that I've been describing, you will be well on your way to creating a strong lifeline during the apocalypse and beyond.

---

[1] John F. Cragan, David W. Wright, Chris R. Kasch, *Communication in Small Groups: Theory, Process, and Skills,* Cengage Learning, 7th ed., paperback, 2008.

[2] Scientific management is a theory of management that studies workflows. Its objective is to improve economic efficiency, especially labor productivity. It is an attempt to apply science to the engineering of processes and management.

[3] "Founded in 1920 in Germany, the Bruderhof is an international communal movement of families and single men and women who seek to put into action Christ's command to love God and neighbor. Like the first Christians described in Acts 2 and 4, we feel called to a way of life in which all are of one heart and soul, no one possesses anything, and everything is shared in common. We also draw inspiration from the Anabaptists of the Reformation era who revived the early Christian example of discipleship in full community." http://www.bruderhof.com

[4] Policy and practice for dealing with mental illness in the domination/violence culture is disastrously ineffective. Public opinion is so warped by ignorance, denial, and avoidance that the only two options for "treating" mental illness are medication and incarceration in the penal system.

[5] Compare with the forces and factors implicit in group life. See Cat-Pad.

Afterword

"And how are the children?"

"All the children are well."

—*Masai greeting*[1]

IF YOU'RE OLD ENOUGH to read this, you are old enough to understand the disasters that await the children of the world.

Absent nuclear holocaust, the oceans will rise and populations will be displaced. Fossil fuels will be depleted and large-scale transportation and industry will fade away and finally collapse, and all but the most local of governments will become more and more useless and finally totally dysfunctional.

During those catastrophes, will your children, your children's children, and their children be well?

If you're old enough to read this, you are old enough to make the well-being of the children your top priority during the apocalypse of civilization. You are old enough to be instrumental, if not powerful, in preparing the generations now born and yet to be born to learn and understand all the values and tools to build a new kind of culture and society, a new post-civilized humanity.

I hope I have convinced you that the basic and underlying cause of the disease that is devouring humanity from within and destroying the natural world is the domination/violence system inherent in civilization.

171

I hope I have convinced you that your personal mission is to commit evolutionary suicide. Doing so will enable you to be free of all of the assumptions, values, memes, and rules about how the civilized world works. All of the truths you have assumed were eternal; the ones that have been passed down, generation after generation, for 10,000 years are defunct. They are killing the children and the natural world.

The youngest of our six great-grandchildren was born in October 2014. It is conceivable that he could reach his 86th birthday in October 2100. Should he live that long, he may have lived through nuclear holocaust, the catastrophic consequences of global warming, the total collapse of the fossil fuel industry, and the collapse of the world's economic and political systems. He may have experienced the die-off of much of the world's population including most of his extended family.

Besides having good genes and the blessing of good health, how will he survive all of that?

He will survive only if his parents and grandparents take on the responsibility of creating a new post-civilized human culture. They will have raised their children to build a new world with a new vision of humanity, based not on the memes of civilization, but on the memes of love and trust and the technology and wisdom of our indigenous forebears.

He will survive if his parents and grandparents build clusters of small sharing, self-sustaining communities whose principal raison d'être is the care and nurture of children and the local environment.

The children are now calling you to commit yourself to join in that small yet awesome project.

I wish you well and I regret that my age will not permit me to accompany you for many more years.

Peter

[1] No tribe in Africa was considered to have warriors more fearsome or intelligent than the Masai. The traditional greeting of Masai warriors was "Casserian Engeri." It translates "And how are the children?" It acknowledges the high value the Masai place on the well-being of the children. Even warriors with no children of their own give the traditional answer, "All the children are well." This means that peace and safety prevail; the priorities of protecting the young and the powerless are in place; that the people had not forgotten their reason for being, their proper function, and their responsibilities.

INDEX

www.ingramcontent.com/pod-product-compliance
Lightning Source LLC
Chambersburg PA
CBHW060850280326
41934CB00007B/985